Society at a Glance

OECD SOCIAL INDICATORS

OECD

ORGANISATION FOR ECONOMIC CO-OPERATION AND DEVELOPMENT

ORGANISATION FOR ECONOMIC CO-OPERATION AND DEVELOPMENT

Pursuant to Article 1 of the Convention signed in Paris on 14th December 1960, and which came into force on 30th September 1961, the Organisation for Economic Co-operation and Development (OECD) shall promote policies designed:
- to achieve the highest sustainable economic growth and employment and a rising standard of living in Member countries, while maintaining financial stability, and thus to contribute to the development of the world economy;
- to contribute to sound economic expansion in Member as well as non-member countries in the process of economic development; and
- to contribute to the expansion of world trade on a multilateral, non-discriminatory basis in accordance with international obligations.

The original Member countries of the OECD are Austria, Belgium, Canada, Denmark, France, Germany, Greece, Iceland, Ireland, Italy, Luxembourg, the Netherlands, Norway, Portugal, Spain, Sweden, Switzerland, Turkey, the United Kingdom and the United States. The following countries became Members subsequently through accession at the dates indicated hereafter: Japan (28th April 1964), Finland (28th January 1969), Australia (7th June 1971), New Zealand (29th May 1973), Mexico (18th May 1994), the Czech Republic (21st December 1995), Hungary (7th May 1996), Poland (22nd November 1996), Korea (12th December 1996) and the Slovak Republic (14th December 2000). The Commission of the European Communities takes part in the work of the OECD (Article 13 of the OECD Convention).

Publié en français sous le titre :
PANORAMA DE LA SOCIÉTÉ
Les indicateurs sociaux de l'OCDE

© OECD 2001
Permission to reproduce a portion of this work for non-commercial purposes or classroom use should be obtained through the Centre français d'exploitation du droit de copie (CFC), 20, rue des Grands-Augustins, 75006 Paris, France, tel. (33-1) 44 07 47 70, fax (33-1) 46 34 67 19, for every country except the United States. In the United States permission should be obtained through the Copyright Clearance Center, Customer Service, (508)750-8400, 222 Rosewood Drive, Danvers, MA 01923 USA, or CCC Online: *www.copyright.com*. All other applications for permission to reproduce or translate all or part of this book should be made to OECD Publications, 2, rue André-Pascal, 75775 Paris Cedex 16, France.

FOREWORD

This report aims to serve a growing demand for a concise but comprehensive quantitative overview of social trends and policy developments. However, because of the multitude and variety of policy areas relevant to social development, putting together a synopsis of data in a meaningful framework is no easy task. This initial listing contains 45 social indicators and covers a broad area. The OECD is continuing its efforts, with the active collaboration of experts in its Member countries, to extend the set of indicators and improve their comparability.

The chosen indicators are listed together with general information on sources and definitions; more detailed information is available on the WebPages of the Directorate of Education, Employment, Labour and Social Affairs (*www.oecd.org/els/social*). Most indicators exist in one form or another already; many are included in various OECD publications on a regular basis. Other indicators have been collected on an *ad hoc* basis. No new large-scale data collection exercise was undertaken for the preparation of this volume.

As this report addresses a wide-range of topics it would have been impossible to complete without the contributions of many different people in and outside the OECD Social Policy Division. The list of contributors include: Willem Adema, Roman Arjona, Andrew Devlin, Catherine Duchêne, Stéphane Jacobzone, Jean-Luc Heller, Peter Hicks, Jeremy Hurst, Mark Keese, Gaetan Lafortune, Zeynep Or, Mark Pearson, Véronique Philippon, Peter Scherer, Peter Tergeist and Andrew Thompson. Mark Pearson took the lead in developing the social indicator project, while Willem Adema co-ordinated the production of this initial report on social indicators. It is published under the responsibility of the Secretary-General of the OECD.

TABLE OF CONTENTS

Part I
An interpretative guide

1.	What are social indicators for?	9
2.	The structure of the indicators	9
3.	The use of the indicators	11
4.	Description of the indicators	12
5.	What you can find in this publication	17
Notes		18
Bibliography		19

Part II
OECD social indicators

G1.	National income	22
G2.	Fertility rates	24
G3.	Old age dependency ratio	26
G4.	Foreigners and foreign-born population	28
G5.	Refugees and asylum-seekers	30
G6.	Divorce rates	32
G7.	Lone-parent families	34
A1.	Employment	36
A2.	Unemployment	38
A3.	Jobless youth	40
A4.	Jobless households	42
A5.	Working mothers	44
A6.	Retirement ages	46
A7.	Activation policies	48
A8.	Spending on education	50
A9.	Early childhood education and care	52
A10.	Educational attainment	54
A11.	Literacy	56
A12.	Replacement rates	58
A13.	Tax wedge	60
B1.	Relative poverty	62
B2.	Income inequality	64
B3.	Low paid employment	66

Table of contents

B4.	Gender wage gap	68
B5.	Minimum wages	70
B6.	Public social expenditure	72
B7.	Private social expenditure	74
B8.	Net social expenditure	76
B9.	Benefit recipiency	78
C1.	Life expectancy	80
C2.	Infant mortality	82
C3.	Potential years of life lost	84
C4.	Disability-free life expectancy	86
C5.	Accidents	88
C6.	Older people in institutions	90
C7.	Health care expenditure	92
C8.	Responsibility for financing health care	94
C9.	Health infrastructure	96
D1.	Strikes	98
D2.	Drug use and related deaths	100
D3.	Suicide	102
D4.	Crime	104
D5.	Group membership	106
D6.	Voting	108
D7.	Prisoners	110

Part I
AN INTERPRETATIVE GUIDE

An interpretative guide

1. What are social indicators for?

The *primary* motives which lie behind this listing of indicators is to give insights into two questions:

– What are the social developments in OECD countries?

– Are the responses of society in general and government in particular effective in altering social outcomes?

The first of these requires a broad coverage of social issues. Insofar as social life requires health, education, freedom to develop, resources and a stable basis of social interactions, so must the indicators reflect these various dimensions.

The second is more challenging. Societies try to influence social outcomes, usually through the medium of government policy. The question is: are such actions effective in achieving their aims? Hence, a first step is to compare changes in social outcomes within the extent of social policies. This process cannot of course be used to evaluate whether a particular social programme is effective. Rather, indicators can be used to assess whether and how the broad thrust of policy is addressing important social issues. Social indicators can be used, for example, to indicate where social spending is high relative to other countries and whether outcomes are correspondingly better. They would not, in such circumstances, tell anyone *why* outcomes are poor, but they do "indicate" that there might be a need to think hard about just why this should be the case.

2. The structure of the indicators

The structure applied in this volume falls well short of being a full-scale framework for the collection of social statistics, but nevertheless is more than a straightforward, one- (or possibly two) dimensional listing of social indicators.

Colleagues using indicators in other parts of the OECD have used different ways in which to assess policy response indicators against policy outcome indicators, and their experience has provided some guidance as to how we might achieve this. For example, the set of education indicators published in *Education at a Glance – OECD Indicators* is implicitly structured into a three part grouping: context; inputs (including expenditure); and outputs (OECD, 2000). Indicators on Science and Technology have been grouped among broad themes such as the globalisation and economic performance and competitiveness to benchmark knowledge-based economies (OECD, 1999).

The Environment Directorate uses yet a different approach in its set of Environmental Indicators (OECD, 2000*a*). The underlying structure of these indicators is based on a model known as a "PSR" framework.[1] In the environmental area:

Human activities exert *pressures* on the environment and affect its quality and the quantity of natural resources *(state)*; society responds to these changes through environmental, general economic and sectoral policies and through changes in awareness and behaviour *(societal response)*. The PSR model has the advantage of highlighting these links, and helping decision-makers and the general public see that environmental and other issues are interconnected.

An interpretative guide

Examples of *pressures* include indirect pressures (indicators of sectoral activities such as energy, transport, industry, agriculture, etc.) and direct pressures (pollutant and waste generation, resource use). Examples of the *state* of the environment are measures of air, water, land quality, ecosystem health, etc. Examples of *responses* include various measures of the extent of policy interventions for environmental purposes (such as expenditure, environmental taxes, etc.). The attraction of the approach is that it focuses on broad indicators of what government and society do (response indicators) with broad indicators of what they are trying to influence (state and pressure indicators).

A similar *approach* of dividing indicators into three categories is followed in this grouping of social indicators. However, the three groupings differs somewhat from the pure PSR model:[2]

- **Social context**. These are those social variables which are not usually directly the target of policy, or which may be policy objectives, but only in the longer term. Nevertheless they are crucial for understanding the context within which social policy is developed. For example, the proportion of people over 64 years of age in the total population is not the target of policy. However, developments in this ratio are of importance in understanding more immediate developments (the living standards of the elderly, for example).

- **Social status**. These are, to the greatest possible extent, descriptions of those social situations that are of highest current priority for policy action. Ideally, the indicators chosen are such that the variables are easily and unambiguously interpreted – all countries would rather have low poverty rates than high ones, for example.

- **Societal response**. These indicators illustrate what society is doing which may affect social status indicators. Most such actions will be government policies, but wider definitions of societal actions might sometimes be useful, as for example, indicators of the activities of non-governmental organisations in the social sphere; the development of private pension saving insofar as this is an important pillar of retirement income policy; and actions taken by individuals and families caring for elderly and young children. However, as data on government policy is generally of better quality than data on societal responses more generally, the initial listing below focuses almost exclusively on the role of the public sector.

Whilst broadly adopting the three-fold approach outlined above, it is not always straightforward to make the distinction between *context* and *status* in the social sphere. For example, fertility is an objective of pro-natalist policies in some countries, but is in the social policy background in others. Similarly, family breakdown can be seen as a failure of public family-support policies in some countries, whereas this would not be an explicit public policy concern in other countries. Regardless of the national policy objectives, family breakdown contributes to growth in the number of families at risk of economic insecurity. Inevitably any dividing line is arbitrary.

2.1. Choosing indicators in view of data considerations

The OECD has 30 countries which vary substantially in their collection of statistics. In choosing the indicators, a choice has to be made as to whether only to include indicators which are already available for all countries or, if not, how significant a departure from this principle should be allowed.

The indicators presented here are not confined to those for which there is absolute comparability across countries. Such a condition would, for example, rule out most income distribution and poverty statistics. Instead, the nature and extent of bias in comparisons between countries is indicated in the sourcing and description of data. This should alert users to potential pitfalls.

As a general rule the list includes only those indicators where there is a reasonable probability of collecting data for at least half of OECD countries. However, this rule is relaxed in some circumstances:

- Where there are known limitations in widely available data, supplementary indicators which illustrate the limitations of the main indicators are included. Such reasoning explains, for example, the including of measures on *net social expenditure*, and the *number of households with no working-age adult in employment,* even though such indicators are available for only a minority of countries.

– The increasing use of longitudinal data sets allows for much more revealing indicators of social status by policy area. The distributions of the duration of unemployment or non-employment spells; the mean length of time spent on particular benefits; the duration of poverty spells are *dynamic* measures of population status. Although only available for a sub-group of countries, these will help give a more rounded picture than is possible if only static cross-sectional data are used.

2.1.1. Disaggregation and measurement

Aggregate data are often decomposed into sub-categories, such as, age group, family type, gender, etc. Use of individual or household data varies according to indicator. However, decompositions for sub-national regions or units of government are not included in this volume; the Territorial Development Service within the OECD is developing a framework for such indicators.

No attempt is made to record all data in the same common units: indicators are presented in a mixture of head counts, currency units, percentages of GDP, etc.

3. The use of the indicators

The *social context* and *social status* measures in themselves describe the social conditions of the population. The *social status* indicators can also be interpreted as measuring one particular dimension of what social policy is aiming to do. Response measures give one (or more) dimension of the scale and nature of social policy interventions. Confronting *response* indicators with *status* indicators provides a first-order indication of policy effectiveness. It is not intended that there should be a "one-for-one" relationship between *societal response* and *social status* indicators. But merely to consider that if the indicators have been chosen well and the measures of *societal response* are high compared to average and the indicators of *social status* low, then there is justification for questioning why there is an apparent anomaly.

Social context indicators are included to help in interpretation of policy effectiveness. Such indicators are intended to enumerate those quasi-exogenous variables which "explain" some part of the *social status* indicators, regardless of the response indicators. Thus, the intention of *social context* indicators is to give some impression of the differences across countries within which public policy operates. Unlike *status* and *response indicators,* it cannot be said about context indicators that a particular outcome is good or bad. For example, where it is easy to say that the less accidents the better, such a statement cannot be made about the number of lone-parent families, while their incidence is clearly a factor which is important to social policy-makers.

Some sort of underlying grouping of indicators into very broad policy fields may well prove useful. In this volume four underlying *objectives* of social policy are used to classify *status* and *response* indicators:

A. Enhancing **self-sufficiency** has been increasingly stressed as an underlying objective of social policy, featuring prominently in, for example, the Communiqué of Social and Health Policy Ministers (OECD, 1999*a*). Autonomy (of individuals or families) is promoted by ensuring active participation in the economy and society, and self-sufficiency in activities of daily living.

B. **Equity** in this context refers mainly to equity of outcome (policies which seek to overcome social or labour market disadvantage, thereby promoting equality of opportunity, are here classified as having as a primary function the promotion of autonomy). Equitable outcomes are measured mainly by the access of households to resources.

C. The underlying objective of **health** care systems is to improve the health status of populations, which leads to a broader focus than an emphasis on disease and its cure, including other social factors which can affect mortality and morbidity.

D. **Social cohesion** is often identified as an over-arching objective of the social policies of countries, but its definition is rarely attempted and there is no cross-country agreement on what precisely it means. However, it is possible to identify various pathologies which have been mentioned as causes of the lack of social cohesion, which do have resonance as objectives of social policy, albeit not ones where cause-and-effect of social policies is straightforward. This is true, for example of crime rates, industrial strife, and family stability.

An interpretative guide

To the extent that responses have an impact on multiple areas of social policy, they can be recorded as relevant indicators in more than one of these broad headings. The ability to undertake activities of daily living without assistance is both a sign of autonomy, and of health; and drug use may signal lack of social cohesion as well as being linked with healthy living. The problem of indicators which could be classified under many different headings is not a problem particular to social policy.[3] The response in other indicator listings is to indicate which indicators would be included in a *comprehensive* listing under each heading, but not to publish the indicator more than once in each publication (see below).

4. Description of the indicators

The chosen indicators are listed below together with general information on sources and definitions. Most indicators exist in one form or another already; many are published in various OECD publications on a regular basis. The majority of the indicators are drawn from underlying databases, often those where co-operation between international organisations is taking place (*e.g.* Labour Force Statistics, Social Expenditure Database). Other indicators have been collected on an *ad hoc* basis, as for example, information on older people in institutions. No new large-scale data collection exercise was undertaken for the preparation of this volume.

It appears that there are far fewer good-quality *response* indicators than social situation indicators. This might be taken as suggesting a need for more effort in improving data collection describing public and private action; including private social spending and information on numbers of people and households receiving different benefits and services from employers and NGOs.

4.1. Context indicators

When comparing social *status* and societal *response* indicators, it is easy to end up making statements that one country is apparently doing badly relative to other countries, or that another is spending a lot of money on something compared with others. It is often important to put such statements into a broader context. For example, national income levels vary across OECD countries. If there is any link between income and health, it might be expected that richer countries have better health status than poor ones. If purchase of health care services is income elastic (as it appears to be) then again, there might be an expectation that rich countries spend more on health care (as a percentage of GDP) than do poorer countries. This does not mean that the indicators of health status and health spending are wrong or misleading. It does mean, however, that there is a simple and easily told story behind the data that should be borne in mind when considering the implications of the indicators.

Many context indicators are of relevance in interpreting a number of other indicators included in this publication. This is true of income per capita, of course, which has implications for the quality, quantity and nature of the social protection which individuals desire. Therefore, context indicators are not categorised as particularly important for understanding trends in any of the four underlying objectives of social policy – equity, autonomy, health or cohesion. Apart from national income (G1), the chosen indicators generally reflect long-term demographic trends and trends in household composition. Throughout the remainder of this volume, the code in-between brackets (*e.g.* G1) refers to an indicator as listed in the tables below. No particular meaning should be attached to the numbering, but this practice simplifies cross-reference purposes.

Context indicators are the following:

G1. National income

G2. Fertility rates

G3. Old age dependency ratio

G4. Foreigners and foreign-born population

G5. Refugees and asylum-seekers

G6. Divorce rates

G7. Lone-parent families

4.2. Self-sufficiency

All systems of social security rely for their funding on contributions by people in work. Most systems in the OECD area encourage this by tying eligibility for social insurance benefits to employment and/or contributory records. Hence, self-sufficiency for the majority of the population of working age is necessary for the very survival of social security. Work (A1, A2) also provides a focus and forum for social interaction, social status and job-satisfaction and is often the focal point for future aspirations.

Social systems have been found to sometimes inadvertently reduce direct financial incentives to work for groups of workers (A12) while at the same time raising labour costs (A13). Hence, social protection systems have to take account of the concomitant tax burden on labour, to avoid adversely affecting labour demand, whilst ensuring that work continues to pay (Pearson and Scarpetta, 2000).

Nevertheless, providing the means to support oneself and one's dependants is sometimes an aspiration rather than a reality (A4). Female labour force participation rates vary sharply across countries, reflecting both social differences and the effectiveness of government policies to overcome the barriers to work which women face (A5). Such problems can be particularly severe for lone parents, who must balance the need for time to care for their families with the need to use that time to earn enough to support them financially. Long-term unemployment is – still – at high levels in many countries, signalling a drift away from an ability to participate in mainstream society. The difficulties which young people face in making the transition from school to work – from being supported to being independent – are considerable in a number of countries (A3).

Whilst indicators of all these elements of employment as a way to achieve independence can be found, many others are absent (at least on an international basis). For example, employment rates of the disabled, "original peoples" and recent migrants are known to be relatively low, but we cannot (yet) give reliable measures of their situation on an internationally comparable basis.

The labour market has turned against low-skilled workers, who in all countries are more likely to find themselves unemployed, non-employed or earning lower wages than their better-educated colleagues. Hence, helping individuals to fulfil their potential requires education from an early age (A9), and indeed throughout the life course. Across the OECD, the societal policy response is geared towards improving general education and literacy standards (A8, A10 and A11), supplemented with specific activation programmes and tax facilities to help the unemployed to find gainful employment (A7, B8). Indeed, the avowed policy objective of social protection systems in OECD countries involves a focal shift from passive benefit delivery to a more active approach geared towards getting benefit recipients into jobs (A7, B6).

Self-sufficiency indicators[1, 2]

Social status		Societal responses	
A1.	Employment	A7.	Activation policies
A2.	Unemployment	A8.	Spending on education
A3.	Jobless youth	A9.	Early childhood education and care
A4.	Jobless households	A10.	Educational attainment
A5.	Working mothers	A11.	Literacy
A6.	Retirement ages	A12.	Replacement rates
		A13.	Tax wedge
		B6.	*Public social expenditure*
		B7.	*Private social expenditure*
		B8.	*Net social expenditure*
		C6.	*Older people in institutions*

1. Italicisation of indicators means that the relevant indicator is not just a self-sufficiency indicator, but that it is also presented in another sub-section.
2. The list of indicators is affected by data availability. For example, in addition to "Jobless households", ideally the variable "Labour force status of households with at least 2 adults of working age" would also have been included (OECD, 1998). However, absence of information for non-European countries means that the variable does not meet the criteria for "good indicators" as given in Section 2.1. Attempts will be made to determine whether suitable other indicators of "work-rich/work-poor" households can be developed other than the household non-employment rate included.

An interpretative guide

Later on in life, work becomes less essential as a means of financial support in view of the public and private pension programmes to which recipients often contributed during their working life (A6, B6, and B7). Indicators of the importance of such spending are discussed in the subsequent section on *equity*. But across OECD countries much policy attention is given to ensuring that elderly persons can maintain their independence and dignity to the greatest extent possible in advanced old age (C6).

4.3. Equity

There are very many dimensions of equity including access, opportunity, and outcome. And within and across societies there are likely to be a multitude of opinions as to exactly what a *fair* redistribution of resources entails or what establishes a *just* distribution of access opportunities to social services. In view of these differences, it is not surprising that it is hard to obtain comprehensive information on all aspects of *equity*. Data limitations are compounded by the fact that social services are often delivered by lower tiers of governments and non-government organisations, which makes it even harder to obtain indicators on, for example, the accessibility of social services to households. Finally, for some services, as for example childminding, households often turn to an informal network of family members and friends, on the prevalence of which no comparable information is available. Hence, the equity *status* indicators are necessarily limited to indicators on financial inequality and "unequal" labour market outcomes (B4).

The development of indicators on financial inequality (B2), and relative poverty (B1), within which earnings (B3) is the most important component, is affected by cross-country differences in national definitions and measurement techniques. The data on income distribution arise out of studies on poverty undertaken by the OECD in recent years, involving the development of a consistent methodology (Förster, 2000, and Oxley *et al.*, 2000).

Apart from labour legislation aimed at safeguarding the position of low-paid workers (B5), social protection systems are the main tool through which policy-makers pursue social policy aims. Regardless, of the national notion on what establishes a fair social service delivery or equitable income support, all OECD countries have developed – or are in the process (OECD, 2000*b*) – social protection systems that to a varying extent redistribute resources within societies (B6). In addition, households may have access to social benefits provided through the private sector (*e.g.* employers and NGOs) or through the tax system (B7 and B8).[4] The magnitude of social systems is further indicated by the number of recipients of publicly controlled social benefits (B9), which when compared to actual workers raises concerns about the financial sustainability of social systems in the long run.

Relative poverty (B1), restricted access to health and other social services, and low levels of literacy and educational attainment (A10, A11) are strongly correlated with each other and the labour market position of the individual and his/her family members (A2, A4, B3). The current distribution of work within societies raises adequacy concerns for groups of families and in particular the children in these families (A9). In recognition of

Equity indicators[1]

Social status	Societal responses
B1. Relative poverty	B5. Minimum wages
B2. Income inequality	B6. Public social expenditure
B3. Low paid employment	B7. Private social expenditure
B4. Gender wage gap	B8. Net social expenditure
A2. *Unemployment*	B9. Benefit recipiency
A3. *Jobless youth*	A7. *Activation policies*
A4. *Jobless households*	A8. *Spending on education*
A5. *Working mothers*	A9. *Early childhood education and care*
	A10. *Educational attainment*
	A11. *Literacy*
	A12. *Replacement rates*

1. Italicisation of indicators means that the relevant indicator is not just an equity indicator, but that it is also presented in another sub-section.

An interpretative guide

the fact that on an individual basis getting work is the most effective tool towards obtaining a more equitable distribution of resources, there is a need for an employment-oriented social policy. There are, however, different approaches to this objective. Interventions at key points of the lifecourse – before and during formal education (A9, A10), during the transition from school to work (A3), in supporting those balancing paid work and caring activities (A5) – can all be effective in preventing disadvantage. A comprehensive and complex set of policies, covering social support, cash benefits and labour market services is required to help people find paid employment. Income support programmes for the non-disabled working age population have been re-focused in many OECD countries towards the reintegration of benefit recipients into the labour market. Direct financial incentives to work have been strengthened (A12). New employment-conditional social benefits have been introduced. Benefit-receipt has been made conditional on job-search activities for a larger group of clients, and sometimes involves mandatory participation in work-placement and training programmes. Finally, benefit administration has been reformed and often involves case-management of clients on an individual basis providing tailored employment support measures towards labour market reintegration.

Equity indicators cannot always be disentangled from self-sufficiency indicators. Taken together, they reveal how national social protection systems grapple with a recurrent social policy dilemma: how to balance adequacy of provisions with sustainability of the overall system and the promotion of individual self-sufficiency?

4.4. Health

There are strong links between social status and health. It is among the poorer countries and the most disadvantaged groups in society (B1), the least educated (A9, A10) or unemployed (A2), that the greatest concentration of morbidity is found and, often, the shortest longevity. As a result, health status of some categories of the population has not improved, and it may have worsened, even while overall there have been improvements in most indicators. Indeed, the growth in living standards, accompanied by better access to health care and continuing progress in medical technology, has contributed to a significant improvement in health status, regardless of whether the indicator used is life expectancy at birth or at any other age; infant mortality; or reduction in infant mortality (C1, C2, and C3).[5]

Improved technology and stricter safety regulations also contribute to a reduction of work- and traffic-related fatality-rates (C5), whilst at the same time growing prosperity has made car-ownership accessible to nearly all, thereby increasing the risk of car-accidents.

The growth in older populations increases the share of those groups in the population which are at risk of a frail health status, not because of age itself but because of a greater incidence of disease and disability at this age. The disability-free life expectancy indicator (C4) can be used to assess whether gains in life expectancy result in extra years lived without disability. And although there is no standardised definition as to how it is measured, the indicator seems to reveal that the population of Member countries can expect to have a significant number of years in good health.

Health indicators[1]

Social status	Societal responses
C1. Life expectancy	C6. Older people in institutions
C2. Infant mortality	C7. Health care expenditure
C3. Potential years of life lost	C8. Responsibility for financing health care
C4. Disability-free life expectancy	C9. Health infrastructure
C5. Accidents	A9. *Early childhood education and care*
B1. *Relative poverty*	A10. *Educational attainment*
A2. *Unemployment*	
D2. *Drug use and related deaths*	

1. Italicisation of indicators means that the relevant indicator is not just a health indicator, but that it is also presented in another sub-section.

© OECD 2001

An interpretative guide

Social trends (higher education levels, easier access to information on medicine) have led to patients calling for better quality health care and a greater say in clinical decisions. Aged individuals may sometimes have difficulty in performing all the activities necessary in daily life, but many elderly prefer not to be institutionalised and would rather stay in their own homes (C6).

Adequacy in access to health care is also affected by insufficient medical insurance coverage or co-payments which prove to be an effective barrier to seeking medical help.[6] Organisation of financing health systems (C8) thus points to the risk of non-coverage. Health care expenditure (C7) and the incidence of medical provisions such as doctors, beds, etc. (C9) reveal the policy response of health care systems to adequacy concerns. Nevertheless, it is important to realise that health care systems have difficulty resolving policy challenges that arise from problems outside the health care system. Where a decline in health status is caused by interrelated social conditions such as unemployment and inadequate housing, health care policies alone cannot suffice.

4.5. Social cohesion

Simultaneously combating social exclusion and promoting social cohesion are regarded as central social policy goals in many OECD countries. However, there is no commonly accepted definition of either social cohesion or social exclusion, which makes identifying suitable indicators all the more difficult. The approach taken in this volume is to present indicators which identify to some degree the extent to which citizens participate in "societal life", or in some way reflect on the strains put on family relationships and relationships between different groups within society. It has proven difficult to find good indicators on the nature of relationships between different societal groups, and only one indicator appears available on a comprehensive basis; the extent to which employment conflicts between unions and employers result in industrial action such as strikes (D1).

Without revealing whether a particular status is "good" or "bad", *context* indicators (Section 2) describe the social condition of the population, and as such point to the existence of different groups and households within society. For example, a high incidence of lone-parenthood (G7) and high divorce rates (G6) are usually considered as "bad", but may be unavoidable (widowhood) or preferable to the alternative (a bad marriage).[7] Not surprisingly therefore these *context* indicators are not subject to avowed policy objectives.

Some measure of societal cohesion can be taken from indicators on the extent with which citizens participate in society, as for example participation in parliamentary elections (D6) and group-membership (D5).

Various indicators help illustrate the lack of social cohesion. Both suicide rates (D3) and drug use and related deaths (D2) point not just to personal breakdown, but also to social conditions. For example, suicide results from many different social and cultural factors: it is more likely to occur particularly during periods of economic, family and individual crisis situations, such as breakdown of a relationship, drinking, drug abuse, and unemployment. Similarly, and although there is much controversy about the causality between crime and social conditions, it is undeniable that crime and fear of crime can destabilise neighbourhoods, and in combination with

Social cohesion indicators[1]

Social status		Societal responses	
D1.	Strikes	D7.	Prisoners
D2.	Drug use and related deaths	A6.	*Activation policies*
D3.	Suicide	A9.	*Early childhood education and care*
D4.	Crime	A10.	*Educational attainment*
D5.	Group membership	B6.	*Public social expenditure*
D6.	Voting	C7.	*Health expenditure*
B1.	*Relative poverty*		
A2.	*Unemployment*		

1. Italicisation of indicators means that the relevant indicator is not just a social cohesion indicator, but that it is also presented in another sub-section.

other social conditions, as for example poverty, leave groups of people in some countries excluded from mainstream society.

It is much more difficult to establish links between the status indicators on social cohesion and relevant response indicators, except and then only to a limited extent between crime (D4) and incarceration rates (D7). Other status indicators are much more difficult to link with policy responses. This is not that surprising as tackling social exclusion involves addressing a multitude of issues captured in the sections on self-sufficiency, equity and health. Fostering social cohesion requires an integrated approach towards pursuing economic, social, health and educational policies.

5. What you can find in this publication

For each indicator, the text describes in a concise manner, the scope and definition of the indicator, what can be discerned from the underlying data and sometimes even more important, what the information cannot be taken to mean, and what measurement problems, if any, may exist. Countries differ in too many ways for it to be possible to pretend that some of the indicators are more precisely defined than they are. There are, inevitably, some differences in data across countries. Where this is the case, the text makes this clear, but also attempts to give some order of magnitude. Hence, for example, our income distribution statistics are not entirely on a standardised basis, so that differences of around 2 points in the indicator chosen should not be seen as necessarily reflecting real differences rather than statistical noise. On the other hand, trends *within* a country over time are usually much more reliable indicators of real change.

The "definition and measurement" section is followed by an "evidence and explanations" section which evidences indicator trends, cross-country differences, and provides some explanation as to why these may occur: this volume does not aspire to describe individual country experiences at length. In general, each indicator contains information for one year available for all OECD countries, and presents trends for a selection of countries. In doing so it also presents information on "composition", *e.g.* gender, age groups, etc., but this varies along with data availability. The text describing each indicator also draws attention to the links between the indicator in question and other *status* and *response* indicators, and each individual indicator contains a "box" with cross-references to other social indicators, not including context indicators. Evidence is presented in charts and tables, and each indicator finishes with a "further reading" section of at most 5 references. Data sources are clearly indicated, with full titles of publications in the further reading section.

5.1. What you can find elsewhere

For the vast majority of indicators, the data underlying the charts and tables can be disaggregated by age of individuals, gender, and family type. There is nearly always a time series of data available. But short of having an extraordinarily long publication, it is not possible to publish all these different dimensions of the indicators collected. However, the raw data underlying each individual indicator is available in the annex on the OECD website (*http://www.oecd.org/els/social*).

5.2. The future

There are possibly many alternative indicators which may better satisfy the aims of this publication. In the immediate future the OECD will focus on improving available indicators concerning benefit recipiency and benefit dependency, long-term care and child well-being. More generally, perhaps we should be identifying what information is "missing" – for example, on the accessibility of basic social services, or the quality of housing.

We would welcome your comments on how we should develop social indicators in the future. Please send them to: OECD, The Social Indicators Project, Social Policy Division, 2, rue André-Pascal, 75775 Paris Cedex 16, France.

Notes

1. The PSR framework is in turn a variant of an approach which has also given rise to the *Driving force – State – Response* (DSR) model used by the UN Committee for Sustainable Development; and the *Driving force – Pressure – State – Impact – Response* (DPSIR) model used by the European Environment Agency.
2. In the environmental indicators, pressure indicators are flow data (emissions, waste generation, and resource use) which affect "stocks" of environmental goods (water or air quality, bio-diversity). Public responses may target both the flows and the stocks. There is no corresponding analogy in social policy. Whilst it is no doubt possible to separate flow and stock data ("flows onto benefit", "number of people on benefit at any one point in time"), this will not always be true for all possible policy areas, and the issues upon which such data would shed light can often be addressed more directly using longitudinal data.
3. For example, emission of some airborne pollutants is a key indicator determining the quality of air, land *and* water resources (OECD, 2000*a*).
4. The data are incomplete and methodologies are still being refined. Nevertheless, the existing partial data are sufficiently interesting to justify the conclusion as an attempt to quantify an increasingly important societal intervention.
5. Given the extensive set of health indicators already published by the OECD, there seems little purpose served by having a large subset reproduced in this volume (OECD, 2000*c*).
6. Insufficient medical services in some geographical regions can also lead to implicit rationing to which better regional planning may offer solutions. However, regional indicators are outside the remit of this volume.
7. Divorce rates in themselves are only a highly imperfect indicator of family stress. It is intended that the indicator of formal divorce be supplemented with indicators of legal separation and, subject to data availability, differentiated by the presence or not of children.

Bibliography

FÖRSTER, M. (2000),
"Trends and driving factors in income distribution and poverty in the OECD area", Labour Market and Social Policy Occasional Paper, No. 42, OECD, Paris.

OECD (1998),
Employment Outlook, Paris.

OECD (1999),
Science, Technology and Industry Scoreboard, Benchmarking Knowledge-based Economies, Paris.

OECD (1999*a*),
A Caring World: the New Social Policy Agenda, Paris.

OECD (2000),
Education at a Glance – OECD Indicators, Paris.

OECD (2000*a*),
Towards Sustainable Development: Environmental Indicators, Paris.

OECD (2000*b*),
Pushing Ahead with Reform in Korea, Labour Market and Social Safety-net Policies, Paris.

OECD (2000*c*),
OECD Health Data 2000, Paris.

OXLEY, H., T. THANH DANG and P. ANTOLIN (2000),
"Poverty dynamics in six OECD countries", *OECD Economic Studies*, No. 30, 2000/1.

PEARSON, M. and S. SCARPETTA (2000),
"What do we know about policies to make work pay?", *OECD Economic Studies*, No. 31, 2000/2, Paris.

Part II

OECD SOCIAL INDICATORS

G1. NATIONAL INCOME

Definition and measurement

Income levels across countries provide an incomplete measure of societal well-being but are crucial to understanding cross-country differences in social status indicators and the scope for societal response.

Gross domestic product measures the size of economies and thus provides an indicator on the level of national income for the resident population, regardless of citizenship. While there are two other different approaches to measuring GDP (adding up all value added by resident producers, or taking the sum of income on labour and capital) only expenditure-based measurement of GDP is available for all OECD countries (OECD, 2000). In this approach the national accounts measures GDP by gross expenditure on the final uses of the domestic supply of goods and services valued at purchasers' values less imports of goods and services (SNA, 1993). Most commonly GDP is measured at market prices including the value of all taxes less subsidies on goods (including imports). Spending indicators that adjust for the impact of the tax system are often related to GDP measured at factor cost as this is net of indirect taxation.

Evidence and explanations

Across OECD countries variation in available resources is substantial. Based on exchange rates, Chart G1.1 shows that average GDP per capita for the three top-ranking countries (Japan, Luxembourg and Switzerland) is more than four times as large as the average for the lowest three countries (Hungary, Poland and Turkey). The highest and lowest income per capita are recorded for, respectively, Luxembourg ($44 360) and Turkey ($2 807).

Comparisons of GDP are arguably best based on **purchasing power parities** (PPP), not market exchange rates. Purchasing power parities reflect the amount of a national currency that will buy the same basket of goods and services in a given country as the US dollar in the United States. When PPPs are taken into account, the differences between poorer countries as, for example, Hungary, Mexico, Poland and Turkey *vis-à-vis* the OECD average diminish.

Data on GDP per capita based on purchasing power parities are available from 1970 onwards, except for the Czech republic, Hungary and Poland (OECD, 2000). **Trends in GDP per capita** show that the OECD unweighted average has increased from about $3 300 in 1970, to about $23 300 in 1999 (Chart G1.2). The unweighted average for the largest 7 economies was about $25 000 per capita in 1999 as compared to $35 000 in the United States. In the last 10 years the US economy has grown particularly rapidly compared with the average of the G7 countries or OECD Member countries more generally. However, fast growth has also taken place in other countries, including Ireland, for example. The Korean economy also grew faster than the OECD average up to 1997, but the severe economic crisis led to a reduction of GDP per capita in 1998.

G1. NATIONAL INCOME

Chart G1.1. GDP per capita in US$, 1999

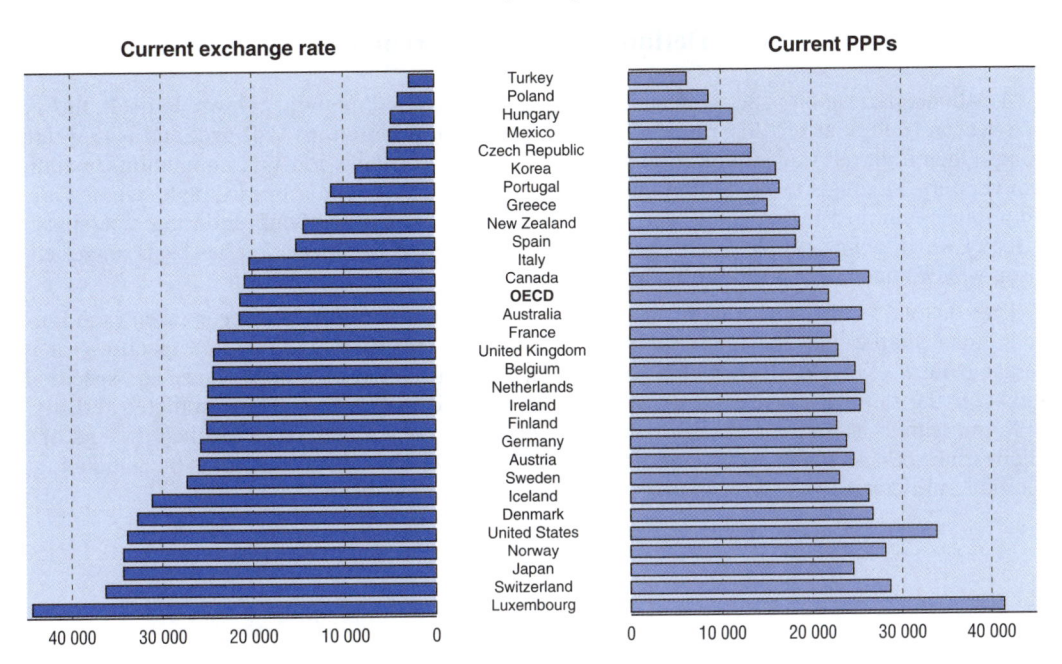

Current exchange rate / *Current PPPs*

Countries (top to bottom): Turkey, Poland, Hungary, Mexico, Czech Republic, Korea, Portugal, Greece, New Zealand, Spain, Italy, Canada, **OECD**, Australia, France, United Kingdom, Belgium, Netherlands, Ireland, Finland, Germany, Austria, Sweden, Iceland, Denmark, United States, Norway, Japan, Switzerland, Luxembourg.

Chart G1.2. GDP per capita for selected countries, 1970-1999
At current prices and current purchasing power parities (US$)

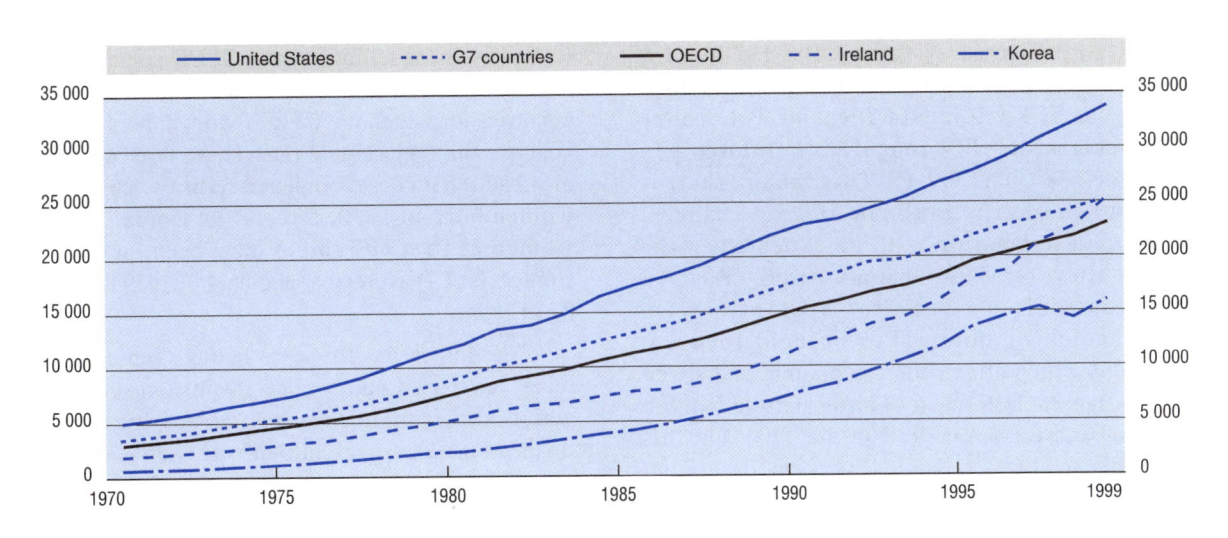

Series: United States, G7 countries, OECD, Ireland, Korea.

Source: OECD (2000).

Further reading

- OECD (2000), *National Accounts*, Paris
- SNA (1993), *System of National Accounts*, CEC-EUROSTAT, IMF, OECD, UN and the World Bank, Brussels/Luxembourg, New York, Paris and Washington DC.

© OECD 2001

G2. FERTILITY RATES

Definition and measurement

A nation's population is determined by fertility, mortality and migratory flows. In itself, this is one good reason to look at fertility rates: if fertility rates fall, populations will age, and if they fall far enough, then high rates of immigration may be necessary to keep a constant population. In addition, however, fertility trends can help illuminate the social state of a country. For example, women are less likely to bear children if they think their future is uncertain, so births often fall during recessions. The difficulty which young people face in getting established in the labour market has been suggested as a reason why women might postpone having their first child.

Data on total fertility rates (TFR) and completed fertility rates (CFR) have been taken from Eurostat and national sources (see the annex on Internet). The total fertility rate (TFR) in a specific year is the average number of children who would be born to a synthetic cohort of women whose age-specific birth rates were the same as those actually observed in the year in question. The completed fertility rate (CFR) measures the number of children that a cohort of women who have reached the end of their childbearing years had in the course of their reproductive life. The CFR is measured by cumulating age-specific fertility rates in a given cohort as they aged from 15 to 49 years.

Evidence and explanations

On average across OECD countries, the **total fertility** rate decreased from 2.4 in 1970 to 1.5 in 1998. Except for Iceland, Turkey and the United States, the TFR fell in OECD countries to below "replacement level" – roughly 2.1 children per woman (see Chart G2.1). This means that, if current age specific birth rates do not change a decline in population is to be expected in the future. However, TFRs that are based on annual birth data often fluctuate substantially as pregnancies are deferred or brought forward, decisions which often reflect economic and social circumstances. Deferment of births until late in life will cause a temporary fall in the TFR, but this will only lead to a fall in CFRs if the deferment results in some births never occurring at all.

Considering age-specific **completed fertility** rates it appears that fertility has fallen amongst younger women in all OECD countries, but is rising amongst older women (Chart G2.2). Nevertheless, CFRs have been falling in most OECD countries, and Australia, Iceland, and Ireland are the only three countries for which the CFR of women born in 1960 is above the replacement rate. These three countries also had the highest completed fertility rates among women born in 1930. Except for Korea, **ages of women at first childbirth** have been increasing, from an OECD average of about 24 in 1970 to almost 27 in 1995.

The fall in fertility rates below "**replacement level**" has raised policy concerns in some countries which have sought to promote fertility through financial incentives or child-oriented services. Other countries do not have avowed public policy objectives towards fertility, although they may nevertheless provide similar family support measures to combat child poverty or to help parents reconcile work and family life.

G2. FERTILITY RATES

Chart G2.1. **Evolution of the total fertility rate for selected countries (1970-1998)**

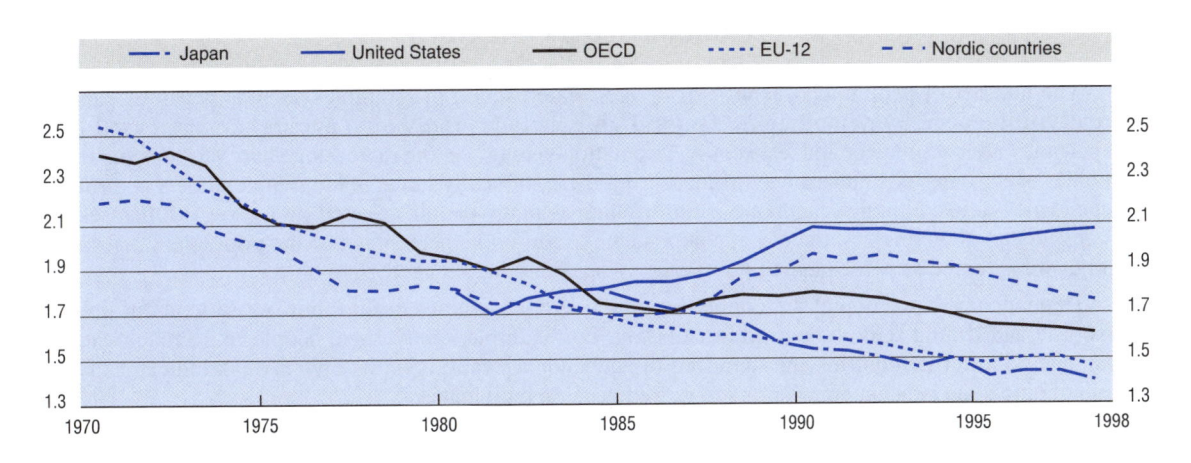

Chart G2.2. **Completed fertility rates for women born in 1930 and 1960 and mean age of women at first childbirth in 1970 and 1995**

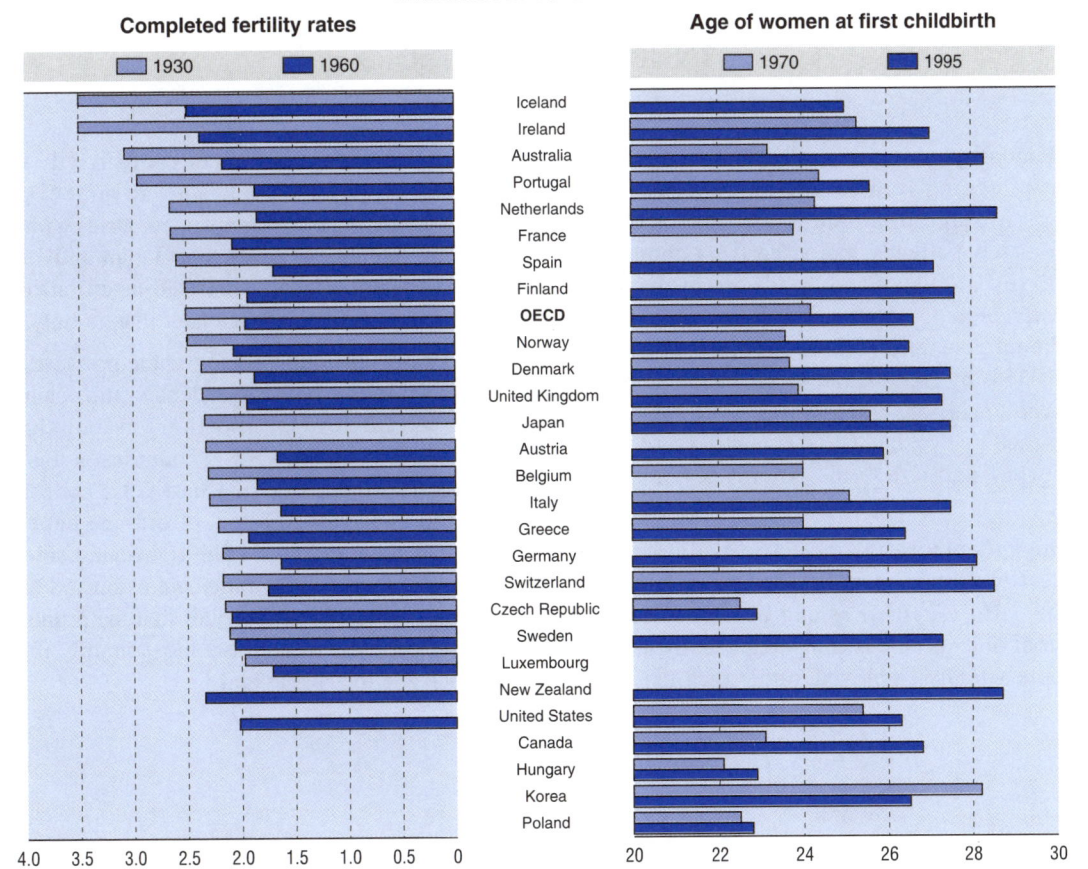

Sources: Eurostat and national sources (see the annex on Internet).

Further reading

- Lestaeghe R. and G. Moors (2000), "Recent trends in fertility and household formation in industrialized world", *Review of Population and Social Policy*, No. 9, pp. 121-170, Tokyo. ■ OECD (1999), *A Caring World: The New Social Policy Agenda*, Paris. ■ OECD (1998), *Family, Market and Community: Equity and Efficiency in Social Policy*, Paris. ■ UN (2000), *Below Replacement Fertility*, New York.

© OECD 2001

25

G3. OLD AGE DEPENDENCY RATIO

Definition and measurement

The number of people who benefit from age-related social programmes such as pensions can be greatly influenced by demographic factors. This includes individual ageing, *i.e.* increased life expectancy after retirement and, especially, population ageing, *i.e.* the increasing share of the population in older age groups. A standard way of measuring these, typically large, demographic effects is through dependency ratios, although the name is unfortunate as many people covered do not regard themselves as dependent. Nevertheless, the old age dependency ratio is the percentage of the population that is 65 and over expressed as percentage of the "working age" population aged 16 to 64.

Dependency ratios depict the context in which ageing policies unfold, but say little about policy response and should seldom be used in isolation. For example, on average, people retire much earlier than age 65 in most countries and therefore the dependency ratio is on its own a weak indicator of the ratio of employed pension contributors to retired pension recipients.

Evidence and explanations

Demographic trends contribute to the pressing nature of ageing-related policy challenges. On average old age dependency ratios in OECD countries have already increased from about 14% in 1960 to 20% today and trends are projected to increase rapidly in about a decade's time when the baby boom generation reaches retirement age and reaches 36% by 2030 (Chart G3.1, Panel A). There are large variations across OECD countries, as exemplified by "young" OECD countries as Mexico and Turkey and two "old" countries (Italy and Japan).

Dependency ratios, taken in isolation, can underestimate pressures on retirement income systems (B6, B7, B8), as can be seen when the number of older people is compared with the number of people actually employed, rather than the whole working-age population (the "**adjusted**" ratio – Chart G3.1, Panel B). The adjusted ratio is significantly higher. Moreover, countries with similar old-age dependency ratios as Japan and Italy can have substantially different "adjusted ratios" – as people in Japan retire much later than in Italy.

Projected future demographic pressures reflect the speed with which dependency ratios change and their actual levels, and there is considerable heterogeneity among OECD countries in this regard. On the left-hand side of Chart G3.2 countries are ordered countries in terms of old-age dependency ratios as they are today. The right-hand side shows the extent to which the ratios are estimated to rise in coming decades, and indicates that the proportion of elderly people will increase most sharply in Korea, Mexico and the Netherlands.

G3. OLD AGE DEPENDENCY RATIO

Chart G3.1. **Old age dependency and adjusted ratios**

A. Old age dependency ratio projected to 2030 for selected averages

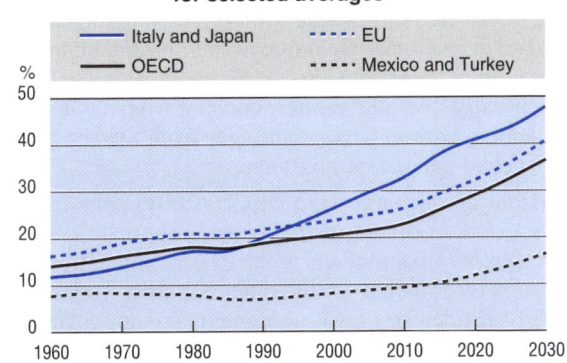

B. Old age dependency and adjusted ratios for Italy, Japan and the OECD average, 1999

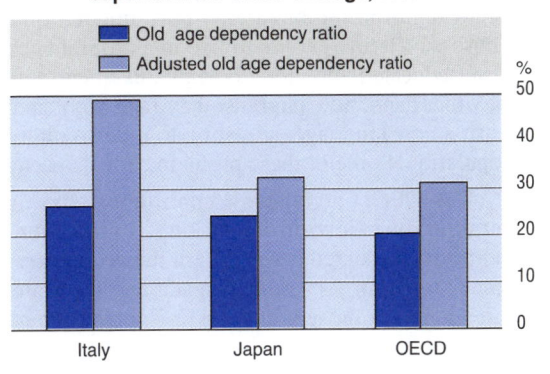

Sources: UN (1999); OECD (2000), *Labour Force Statistics*, Paris.

Chart G3.2. **Old age dependency ratios**

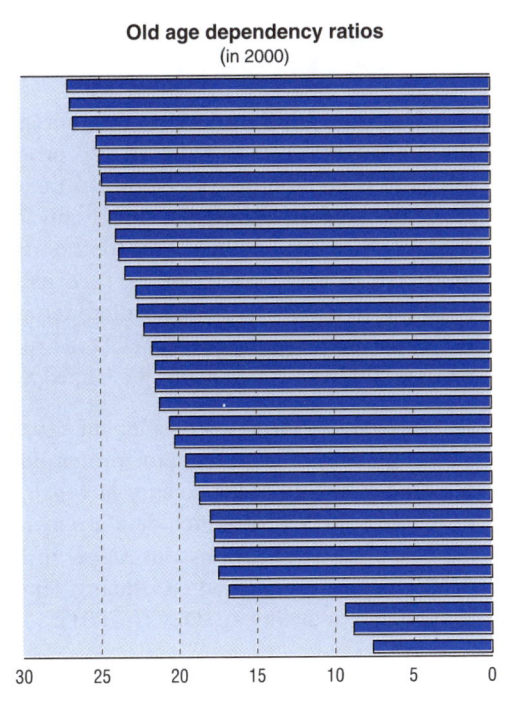

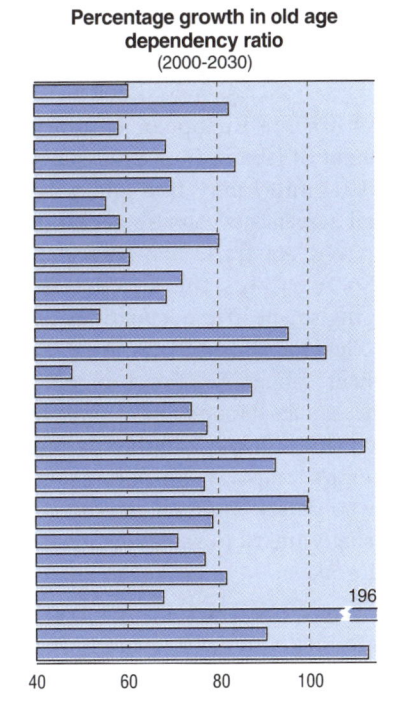

Source: UN (1999).

Further reading

- OECD (2000), *Reforms for an Ageing Society*, Paris. ■ OECD (1998), *Maintaining Prosperity in an Ageing Society*, Paris. ■ United Nations (1999), *World Population Prospects: The 1998 Revision*, New York.

G4. FOREIGNERS AND FOREIGN-BORN POPULATION

Definition and measurement

A high foreign or foreign-born population creates both challenges and opportunities to societies. Those who freely choose to live in a different country and even culture from that of their birth tend to be better educated and more dynamic, even entrepreneurial, than those who choose to remain at home. On the other hand, new migrants may face problems in their daily lives in their new country, from having to learn a new language, adjusting to a new culture, to dealing with any racist attitudes from the resident population. Some of these problems are also acute for second-generation migrants.

The OECD maintains a continuous reporting system on migration and OECD (2001) contains a detailed overview of definitions, sources and measurement discrepancies across countries. The indicators presented here concern the proportion of foreign born populations in the overall population or labour force for Australia, Canada and the United States. Information for the other countries concerns foreigners, *i.e.* those without a passport of the country of residence. Illegal immigrants are not covered in any of the statistics.

Evidence and explanations

Within the European Union there is **free movement** of labour, so in principle people born in one EU country may live and work in another. Bilateral agreements can also permit the free flow of labour (*e.g.* Australia and New Zealand), while NAFTA regulates the movement of workers belonging to specific occupations across Canada, Mexico and the United States. Apart from such "free movement" agreements, most migration into OECD countries comes through one of three routes: asylum-seekers; flows linked with family reunion; and the granting of temporary or permanent residence to those who satisfy immigration criteria, and these are increasingly linked to satisfying demand for highly-skilled workers.

Across the OECD, Australia, Canada, Luxembourg and Switzerland stand out as the countries with high proportions of foreigners and foreign-born populations, both in the population and labour force (Chart G4.1). Japan, Portugal and Finland are at the other end of the spectrum, with foreign labour force participation being particularly low in Japan.

Between 1988 and 1998, the increase in the foreign/foreign-born population as a proportion of the overall population was largest in Luxembourg, Austria, and Switzerland, Denmark and the United States while only France recorded a significant decrease in the proportion of foreigners in its population (Chart G4.2). In absolute terms (see the annex on Internet), the main OECD net recipient of foreign-born residents remains the United States.

Although subject to considerable cross-country variation, about 2-3 per cent of foreign populations acquire nationality of the country in which they live. In most countries for which data are available the number of **naturalisations** was higher in 1998 than in 1995, except for Canada, Germany, Hungary, the Netherlands and Norway (OECD, 2001).

There can be large differences in **fertility rates** between nationals and the foreign (born) residents (the latter being twice the rate of the former in Sweden). However, there is no general tendency towards increasing discrepancy in fertility rates in this regard (OECD, 2001).

G4. FOREIGNERS AND FOREIGN-BORN POPULATION

Chart G4.1. Foreign and foreign-born population in OECD countries, 1998

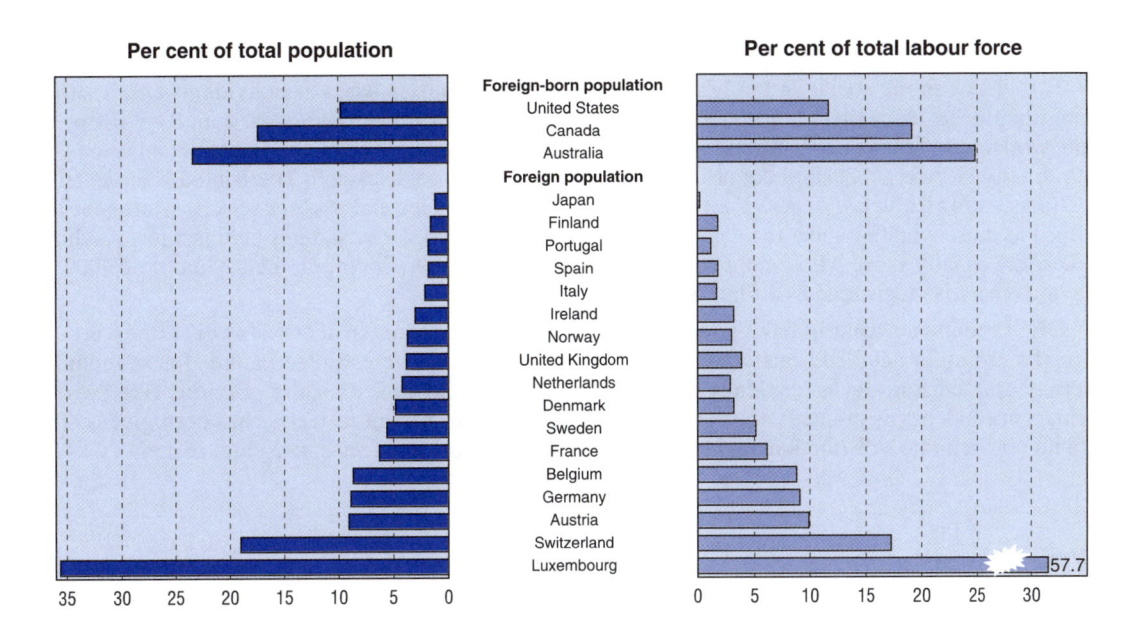

Chart G4.2. Change in the proportion of foreign and foreign-born population, 1988-1998
Percentage points change since 1988

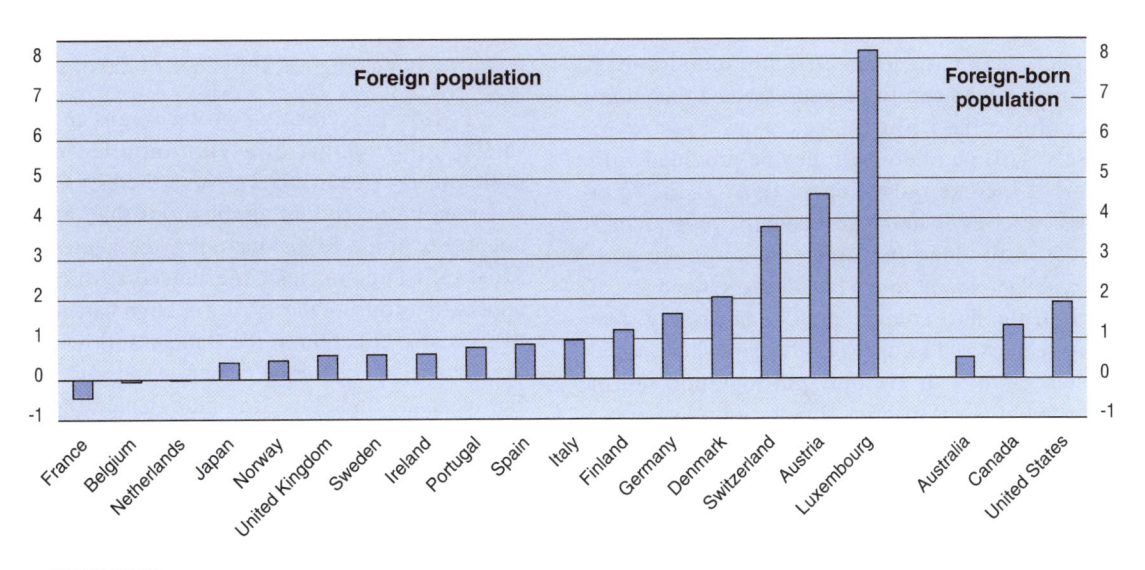

Source: OECD (2001).

Further reading
- OECD (2001), *Trends in International Migration*, Paris.
- United Nations (1999), *World Population Prospects: The 1998 Revision*, New York.

G5. REFUGEES AND ASYLUM-SEEKERS

Definition and measurement

Turbulence in the social and political situation within countries leads to individuals and families being displaced from their homes. Refuge may be sought in other countries, usually within the framework of government programmes, negotiated either with specialised international organisations, or with the (usually neighbouring) countries which are sheltering the displaced. The United Nations High Commission for Refugees oversees arrangements for both refugees and asylum seekers. Refugees are defined as those who fall under the various UN conventions, protocols or statutes on this topic. Asylum-seekers are usually those whose applications for refugee status are pending in the asylum procedure or who are otherwise registered as asylum-seekers.

OECD countries usually have good and detailed data on asylum-seekers. However, they do not normally maintain detailed registers of the refugee population. The estimate included here includes persons granted long-term residency status, based on total inflows over the previous five (where permanent residency is granted) or ten years (where no such permanent residency has been given). The data do not facilitate a distinction between economic and political refugees and asylum-seekers.

Evidence and explanations

Asylum-seekers loom higher in domestic **policy debates** than their absolute numbers might lead one to expect. There are some difficult social policy questions which need to be addressed: do asylum-seekers have the right to seek work to support themselves? If not, how will they be provided with sufficient income on which to live? If they get permission to reside in the host country, programmes to assist in the learning of a new language and, maybe, skills relevant to the labour market and social system of the host country may be necessary. Are asylum-seekers and refugees to live anywhere in the recipient country or are they put together within designated areas, restricting integration in society? Conflicting objectives in designing effective systems of support mean that refugees and recently successful asylum-seekers figure high in lists of the socially excluded in recipient countries.

Among OECD countries, the refugee population makes up more than 1% of the total population in the Nordic countries and Austria, Germany and Switzerland (Chart G5.1). Otherwise, most northern European and non-European OECD countries have 150-400 refugees per 100 000 population, while southern European countries have a significantly lower ratio of refugees.

Following German government measures in 1993, the number of **asylum-applications** fell dramatically (Chart G5.2). Nevertheless, Germany received more asylum applications than any other country over the 1990s, including the United States. Most OECD countries experienced an increase in applications during the 1990s, in large part related to the unstable situation in the Balkan. Inflow ratios of asylum seekers in Nordic countries and some Central European are high, but also in the Benelux countries, Ireland, and the United Kingdom (see the annex on Internet).

What happens to those whose applications have been turned down is a pressing social question. The fate of **unsuccessful applicants** is unknown. Many are thought to still be in the country of application, surviving on family support and activities in the unofficial economy.

G5. REFUGEES AND ASYLUM-SEEKERS

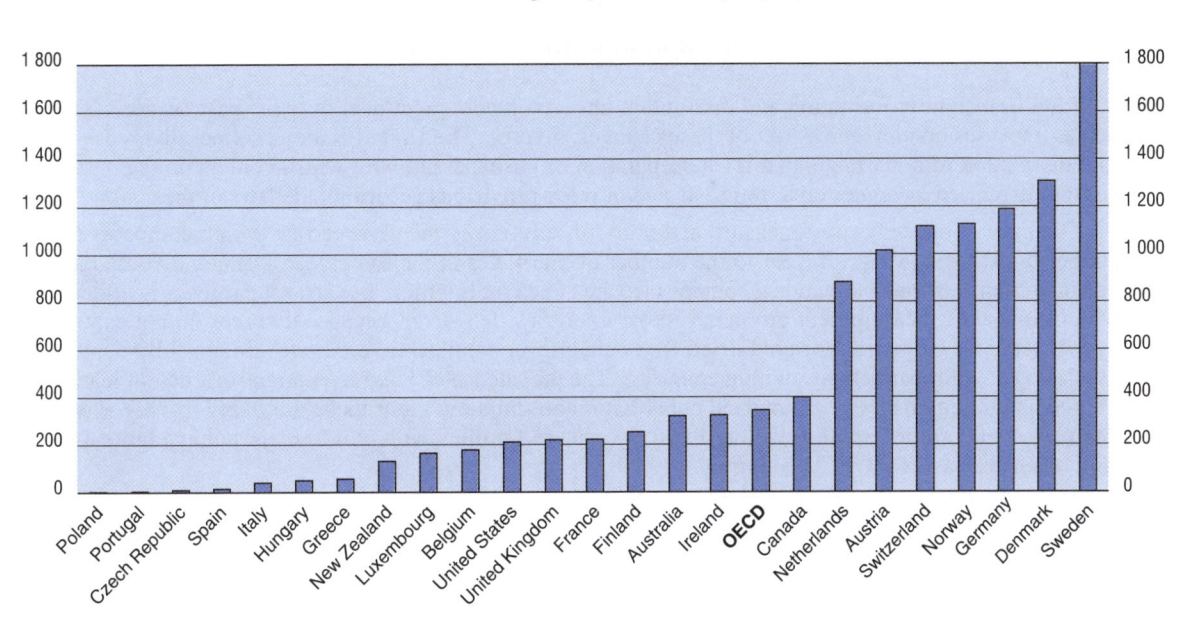

Chart G5.1. **Refugees per 100 000 people, 1999**

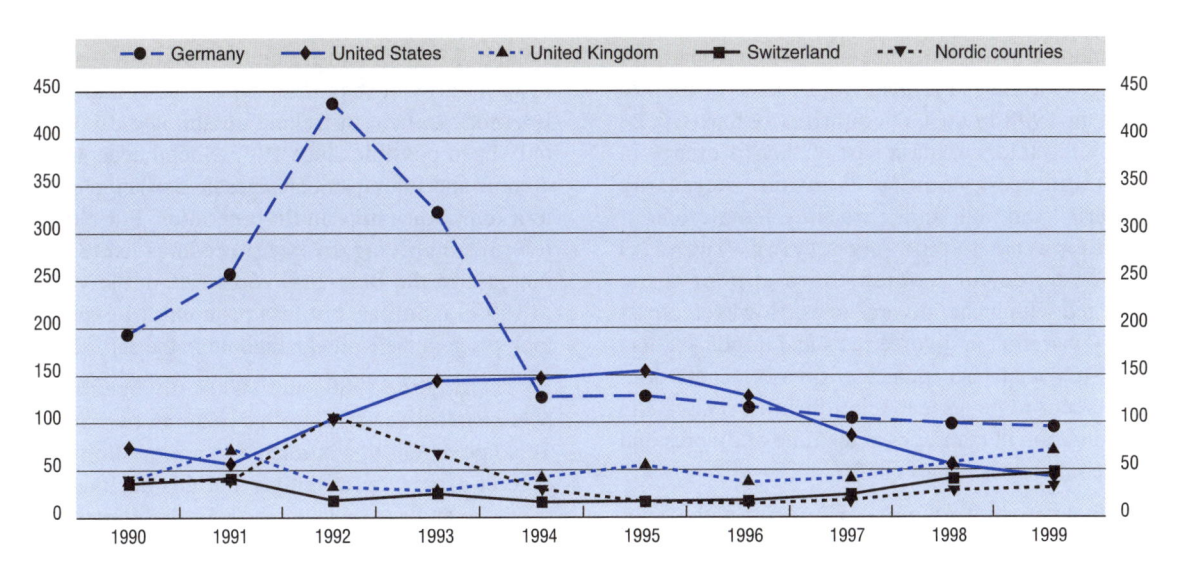

Chart G5.2. **Inflows of asylum-seekers in thousands (1990-1999)**

Source: OECD (2001).

Further reading

- OECD (2001), *Trends in International Migration*, Paris. ■ UN High Commissioner for Refugees (2000), *Refugees and Others of Concern to UNHCR: 1999 Statistical Overview*, Geneva. ■ United Nations (1999), *World Population Prospects: The 1998 Revision*, New York.

G6. DIVORCE RATES

Definition and measurement

Patterns of family formation and dissolution have evolved a great deal over the past decades. This indicator focuses on only one aspect of these changes: divorce. The United Nations defines divorce as "a final dissolution of a marriage, that is, the separation of husband and wife which confers on the parties the right to remarriage under civil, religious and/or other provisions according the laws of the country".

The most commonly-used measure of family dissolution is the divorce rate which compares the number of divorces in a given year to the number of marriages in the same year. Data on divorce rates are taken from Eurostat and national sources (see the annex on Internet), but are not particularly affected by definitional or measurement problems across countries. However, because divorces do not capture legal separations of married or unmarried (but cohabiting) couples, divorce rates do not fully capture dissolution of adult partnerships within countries. The prevalence of legal separations that do not lead to divorce and the incidence of unmarried cohabitation are unknown, but these are likely to vary across countries. Data on the extent to which divorces concern families with children are not available on a comprehensive basis for OECD countries.

Evidence and explanations

For the 24 OECD countries for which data are available, the average divorce rate as a percentage of marriages has almost **tripled** from 14.3% in 1970 to 41.2% in 1998 in OECD countries (Chart G6.1). Economic factors explain part of the difference in trends and cross-country variation. Increasing prosperity and high and increasing female labour market participation signifying financial independence for women, both appear to be associated with higher divorce rates. However, cross-country variation in divorce rates and trends are also related to societal acceptance of divorce. There does not to seem to be a clear relationship between the mean duration of marriages at the time of divorce and divorce rate levels (Chart G6.2).

Divorce rates vary **across countries** with socio-cultural factors. Since the mid-1990s, divorce rates as a percentage of marriages exceed 50% in Belgium, the Czech Republic, Finland, Sweden, and the United Kingdom, while Southern European countries, Korea, Poland, Mexico, and Ireland continue to record the lowest rates at less than 20% (see the annex on Internet). In fact, in Ireland obtaining a divorce has only been possible since 1997. Social acceptance of divorce and subsequent changes in legislation can lead to a temporary hike in divorce rates. For example, reform simplifying divorce procedures led to a rapid increase in the Belgian divorce rate in the years up to 1995: a similar, but less pronounced experience took place in the United Kingdom in the early 1970s.

During the 1980s and 1990s, divorce rates fell over consecutive years in some countries (*e.g.* Sweden). To some extent this is related to a preceding hike in divorce rates (*e.g.* Belgium), but this decline is also related to an increase in unmarried **cohabiting couples**. These *de facto* unions are more common than marriage among younger generations, especially, in the Nordic countries.

G6. DIVORCE RATES

Chart G6.1. **Trends in divorce rate, 1970-1998**

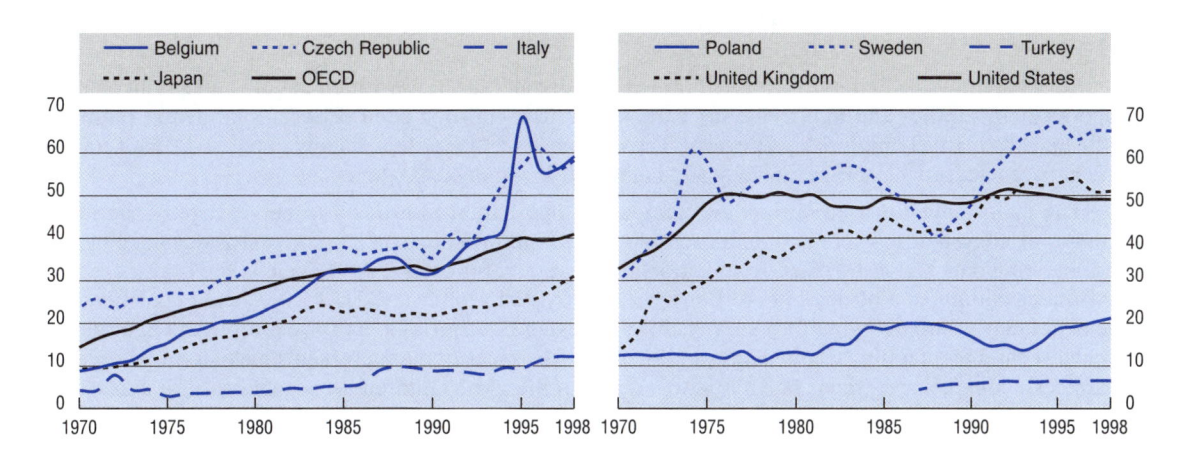

Chart G6.2. **Number of divorces per 100 marriages and mean marriage duration at divorce, 1995**

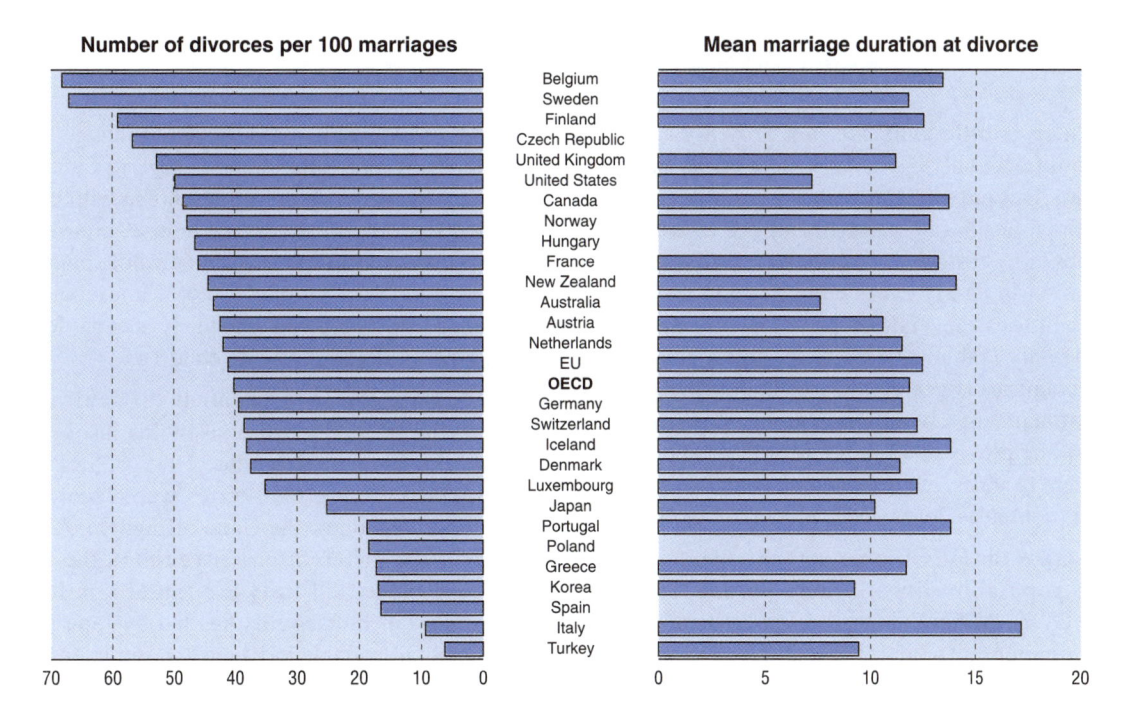

Sources: Eurostat and national sources (see the annex on Internet).

Further reading

- OECD (1998), *Family, Market and Community: Equity and Efficiency in Social Policy*, Paris. ■ Statistics Canada (1998), "Religious Observance, Marriage and Family", *Canadian Social Trends*, Autumn 1998, Ottawa.

G7. LONE-PARENT FAMILIES

Definition and measurement

Lone parents have half as much total time as two-parent families in which to gain enough income to support their families and to provide the care which their children need. Hence, lone-parent families (LPF) face a relatively high risk of poverty. The incidence of LPF within society exposes difficult trade-offs between addressing self-sufficiency and child well-being in social policy.

The main indicator used here is the number of lone-parent families as a percentage of the total number of households. There is no data set that collates information on LPF on a cross-country basis, and therefore data had to be taken from national sources and Eurostat (1999), which, however, does not facilitate a comparison of numbers of households across EU countries. Thus, there exist considerable measurement problems related to survey differences and definitions, as for example the age of the youngest child in a family (see the annex on Internet). The measurement problems make it impossible to establish comprehensive trends on LPF *vis-à-vis* all families with children: trends can only be expressed in annualised growth rates of the proportion of LPF in all households.

Evidence and explanations

There is little evidence that growing up in a household with only one adult is necessarily bad for children. But poverty *can* be bad for children, and lone-parent families (9 out of 10 LPF are lone-*mother* families) are vastly over-represented in the poor population in nearly every country (B1). Being in work reduces the **risk of poverty** among LPF considerably (Table G7.1). Hence, policy reform in many countries is geared towards increasing labour force attachment among lone parents, for example through the provision of more affordable and better child-care facilities, while tightening benefit-eligibility criteria to stimulate lone parents to look for work.

Across the OECD area, only a small minority of the population lives in lone-parent families (Table G7.2). Within Europe, lone-parent families are most common in Ireland, Finland, Norway and the United Kingdom. Outside of Europe data are collected on a different basis, reflecting the number of households, rather than the number of people in those households, but nevertheless indicate that the incidence of lone-parenthood is high in Canada and the US. The proportion of households with children headed by lone parents is, of course, significantly higher than their proportion in the whole population. In Australia, for example, 7.6% of households may be headed by lone parents, but they account for more than 20% of all families with children.

Despite the measurement difficulties, the proportion of LPF in all households has grown in most OECD countries since 1985 (Chart G7.1). Particularly high growth rates were recorded for Belgium, Ireland and the United Kingdom. Although from a very different base, **trends** in the United States, France and Italy are rather similar. The proportion of households headed by lone parents remained fairly stable in Korea and southern Europe. However, this reflects, in part, the general decline in fertility in southern Europe: there are fewer households of whatever composition with children.

G7. LONE-PARENT FAMILIES

Chart G7.1. **Growth in the proportion of lone-parent households in all households: 1985=100**

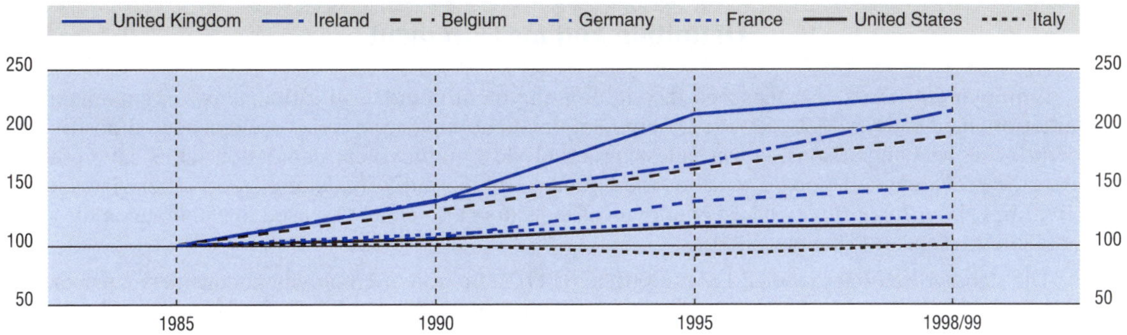

— United Kingdom — · Ireland – – · Belgium – – · Germany ····· France —— United States ····· Italy

Sources: Eurostat and national sources (see the annex on Internet).

Table G7.1. Percentage of persons living in households with incomes below 50% of median adjusted disposable income of the entire population

	Proportion of single parents in work	Poverty rates — Non-working single parents	Poverty rates — Working single parents		Proportion of single parents in work	Poverty rates — Non-working single parents	Poverty rates — Working single parents
Australia, 1994	46	42.1	9.3	Mexico, 1994	89	31.0	27.2
Austria, 1993	64	20.8	8.9	Netherlands, 1995	34	41.3	17.0
Canada, 1995	63	72.5	26.5	Norway, 1995	61	29.6	4.6
Denmark, 1994	74	34.2	10.0	Sweden, 1995	87	24.2	3.8
France, 1994	70	45.1	13.3	Turkey, 1994	45	39.9	16.3
Germany, 1994	57	61.8	32.5	United Kingdom, 1995	47	65.0	22.7
Greece, 1994	59	36.8	16.3	United States, 1995	73	93.4	38.6
Italy, 1993	58	78.7	24.9	**OECD**	**62**	**47.8**	**18.1**

Source: Förster (2000).

Table G7.2. **Composition of households by type of household in 1995**

	One-person households	Couples without children	Couples with children	Lone-parent families	Other households		One-person households	Couples without children	Couples with children	Lone-parent families	Other households
Raw data reflect the proportion of persons living in private households by type of household
Austria	12.0	19.0	54.0	8.0	7.0	Luxembourg	9.0	18.0	55.0	5.0	13.0
Belgium	10.0	20.0	58.0	7.0	4.0	Netherlands	13.0	25.0	56.0	5.0	1.0
Denmark	17.0	26.0	50.0	6.0	2.0	Norway	19.0	20.0	50.0	9.0	2.0
Finland	15.0	21.0	50.0	9.0	5.0	Portugal	4.0	14.0	57.0	8.0	18.0
France	12.0	20.0	56.0	7.0	5.0	Spain	4.0	11.0	61.0	6.0	17.0
Germany	14.0	25.0	50.0	5.0	5.0	Sweden	24.0	31.0	31.0	3.0	11.0
Greece	7.0	16.0	56.0	5.0	16.0	Switzerland	14.0	23.0	54.0	6.0	3.0
Ireland	6.0	9.0	65.0	9.0	11.0	United Kingdom	11.0	22.0	52.0	10.0	6.0
Italy	8.0	16.0	66.0	7.0	3.0						
Raw data reflect the number of households
Australia	24.2	30.5	27.9	7.6	9.8	Japan	22.6	18.4	35.3	5.2	18.5
Canada	24.2	20.7	32.7	10.5	11.8	New Zealand	20.1	27.8	23.6	8.9	19.7
Korea	x	12.6	58.6	8.6	20.3	United States	25.7	28.3	24.6	9.3	12.1

Sources: Eurostat and national sources (see the annex on Internet).

Further reading

■ Eurostat (1999), *Living conditions in Europe*, Brussels/Luxembourg. ■ Förster, M. (2000), "Trends and driving factors in income distribution and poverty in the OECD area", OECD Labour Market and Social Policy Occasional Paper No. 42. ■ OECD (1999), *A Caring World: The New Social Policy Agenda*, Paris. ■ OECD (1998), *Families, Markets and Communities: Equity and Efficiency in Social Policy*, Paris.

A1. EMPLOYMENT

Definition and measurement

Employment levels, as measured through employment/population ratios, show engagement in market-oriented activity (A2). Relatively high employment/population ratios are considered positively in cross-country comparisons. Nevertheless, relatively low employment/population ratios say nothing about the prevalence of unpaid work or the extent to which individuals engage in otherwise social activities. Labour force survey based employment indicators also cannot be used to elaborate on the size of the informal sector (Thomas, 2000).

The standardised International Labour Office (ILO) definition of employment considers a person as employed, if he/she works for pay, profit or family gain (in cash or in kind), for at least one hour per week, or is temporarily absent from a job because of illness, holidays or industrial dispute (D1). The total employment/population ratio presented here is the proportion of the population of working age (all persons aged between 15 and 65) who are self-employed or in paid employment. Part-time employment refers to persons who usually work less than 30 hours per week in their main job. Data are gathered through national labour force surveys.

Evidence and explanations

Trends in employment/population ratios reveal strong employment growth in the OECD and the EU during the second part of the 1990s, after the more lack-lustre 1980s (Chart A1.1, Panel A). Individual country experiences, however, differ sharply. Since the beginning of the 1990s, employment growth has been strong in, for example, Ireland, the Netherlands, and the USA, while Finland, Germany, Korea, Poland and Sweden are among the countries that experienced significant employment reductions at some interval during the 1990s (see the annex on Internet for more details).

At the turn of the millennium, the **level** of the average OECD employment/population ratio was close to 66%. Turkey, Italy and Spain have the lowest employment/population ratios (less than 55%). In the Nordic countries, Switzerland and the US employment/population ratios are in excess of 70% (Table A1.1).

Across the OECD area, female employment/population ratios have increased considerably over the last two decades (Chart A1.2, Panel A), thereby narrowing the "**gender gap**" in employment. Nevertheless, on average across the OECD men are still much more likely to be in employment than women (B4).

On the other hand, women are much more likely to be in **part-time employment** than men (Table A1.1). At least in part, this is because part-time employment makes it easier for mothers to combine work with caring responsibilities for young children. Since young children are present in all countries, other factors must be important in explaining that the prevalence of part-time work varies considerably across countries: in the Netherlands more than 30% of those in employment work on a part-time basis, but this is only about 3.5% in the Czech Republic and Hungary (Table A1.1).

Employment among **older workers** (55-64 years) has declined rapidly since 1970 (A6). On average across the OECD, less than 50% of the older workers were in employment in 1999 while across the EU this is below 40%.

Status indicators: Unemployment (A2), Working mothers (A5), Retirement ages (A6), Low paid employment (B3), Gender wage gap (B4).
Response indicators: Activation policies (A7), Replacement rates (A12), Tax wedge (A13), Minimum wages (B5).

A1. EMPLOYMENT

Chart A1.1. Evolution of the employment/population ratios since 1980

A. Total employment/population ratio (United States, OECD, Germany, EU, Spain)

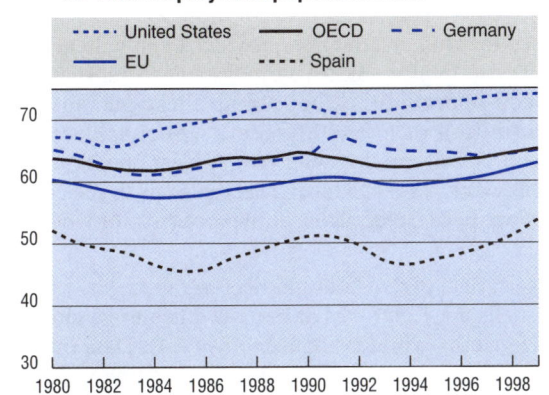

B. Female employment/population ratio (Norway, Canada, Netherlands, OECD, EU)

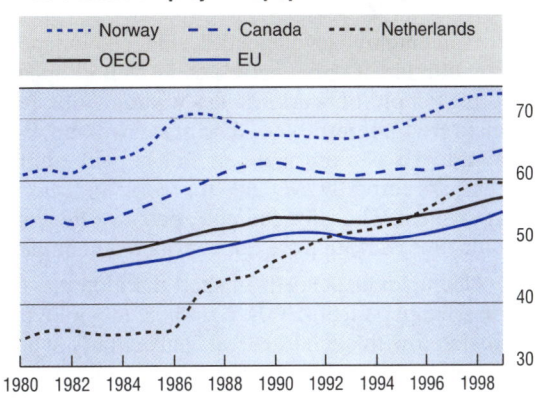

Source: OECD (2000), *Labour Force Statistics*.

Table A1.1. Employment indicators, 1999

	Employment/population ratio (As a percentage)						Incidence of part-time employment (As a proportion of employment)		
	All ages	15-24	25-54	55-64	Men	Women	Total	Men	Women
Turkey	51.9	42.6	57.8	42.6	71.7	32.0	7.1	3.5	15.1
Italy	52.5	25.5	66.9	27.5	67.6	38.3	11.8	5.3	23.2
Spain	53.8	33.9	65.6	34.9	69.6	38.3	7.9	2.9	16.8
Greece	55.6	28.1	69.9	39.1	71.6	40.3	9.0	5.3	15.4
Hungary	55.7	35.7	72.3	19.4	62.6	49.0	3.5	2.1	5.1
Belgium	58.9	25.5	76.4	24.7	67.5	50.2	19.9	7.3	36.6
Poland	58.9	28.6	75.0	32.3	63.6	51.6	11.8	8.0	16.6
Korea	59.7	26.8	70.4	58.1	71.5	48.1	7.8	5.9	10.5
France	59.8	20.8	77.0	34.2	66.8	52.9	14.7	5.8	24.7
Mexico	61.2	50.8	67.8	55.2	84.8	39.6	13.8	7.2	26.9
Luxembourg	61.6	31.7	76.7	26.3	74.4	48.5	12.1	1.6	28.3
Ireland	62.5	46.4	73.2	43.8	73.4	51.3	18.3	7.9	31.9
Germany	64.9	46.8	78.2	38.5	73.1	56.5	17.1	4.8	33.1
Czech Republic	65.9	40.1	81.9	37.5	74.3	57.4	3.4	1.7	5.6
Finland	66.0	38.8	80.3	39.2	68.4	63.5	9.9	6.6	13.5
Portugal	67.3	43.2	80.8	50.8	75.5	59.4	9.3	5.0	14.6
Australia	68.2	60.8	75.4	44.3	76.1	59.3	26.1	14.3	41.4
Austria	68.2	54.9	81.3	29.2	76.6	58.5	12.3	2.8	24.4
Japan	68.9	42.9	78.7	63.4	81.0	56.7	24.1	13.4	39.7
New Zealand	70.0	54.6	77.6	56.9	77.3	63.0	23.0	11.3	37.2
Canada	70.1	54.6	79.2	46.9	75.5	64.7	18.5	10.3	28.0
Netherlands	70.9	62.7	80.6	35.3	79.9	59.4	30.4	11.9	55.4
United Kingdom	71.7	60.8	79.7	49.4	78.4	64.9	23.0	8.5	40.6
Sweden	72.9	43.8	82.6	64.0	74.8	70.9	14.5	7.3	22.3
United States	73.9	59.0	81.4	57.7	80.5	67.6	13.3	8.1	19.0
Denmark	76.5	66.0	84.4	54.2	81.2	71.6	15.3	8.9	22.7
Norway	78.0	57.8	85.5	67.3	82.1	73.8	20.7	8.2	35.0
Switzerland	79.7	64.7	85.2	71.7	87.2	71.8	24.8	7.7	46.5
Iceland	84.2	65.1	90.9	85.9	88.2	80.2	21.2	9.1	35.2
EU	62.6	39.5	75.5	37.8	73.3	55.0	16.4	6.0	30.3
OECD	**65.9**	**46.7**	**75.9**	**48.9**	**75.0**	**56.5**	**15.8**	**7.8**	**26.4**

Source: OECD (2000), *Employment Outlook*.

Further reading

■ OECD (2000), *Employment Outlook*, Paris. ■ OECD (2000), *Labour Force Statistics*, Paris. ■ OECD (2000), *Policies Towards Full Employment*, Paris. ■ OECD (1999), *Implementing the OECD Jobs Strategy: Assessing Performance and Policy*, Paris. ■ Thomas, J. (2000), "The black economy", *World Economics*, Vol. 1, No. 1, Henley-on-Thames, United Kingdom.

© OECD 2001

A2. UNEMPLOYMENT

Definition and measurement

Paid employment engenders financial independence for workers, but also provides them with access to a multitude of social networks, as well as opportunities to improve skills, earnings and social status in future. People of working age without jobs lack such opportunities, but not all these persons are considered unemployed. The standardised ILO definition of unemployment (A1) considers the unemployed as those who: are not in paid employment or self-employment (for at least one hour per week); are currently available for work; and, are seeking work, *i.e.* have taken specific steps to seek paid employment. Thus, for example, people who cannot work because of physical impairments, or who are in full-time education are not considered unemployed.

Unemployment spells of short duration may simply reflect high labour market turnover rates. Long-term unemployment (LTU), *i.e.* when unemployment spells are 12 months or more is much more closely associated with social distress, particularly when it concerns workless households (A4). Data on the unemployment and the long-term unemployment rates, *i.e.* the number of (long-term) unemployed as a percentage of the labour force, are gathered through national labour force surveys.

Evidence and explanations

Trends in unemployment are affected by the changes in economic activity and other factors influencing labour demand (A13, B5), specific labour market characteristics (*e.g.* seasonal employment patterns), demographic factors affecting labour supply, and social programme design (A12, B9). From its post-war high in the beginning of the 1990s, the unemployment rate in the OECD area has declined to around 6½ per cent in 1999 (Chart A2.1, Panel A). **Trends**, however, vary widely. Since the beginning of the 1990s unemployment in the United States has fallen to historically low levels. While unemployment in the EU has also fallen since 1994, it is still above 1990-levels. In contrast, since 1992 unemployment has risen steadily in Japan.

In general, female unemployment trends are similar to overall unemployment trends, albeit at a much higher level in some countries (Chart A2.1, Panel B). On average, the **gender gap** in unemployment rates is less than 1 percentage point across the OECD, but averages nearly 3 percentage points across the EU (Table A2.1).

Unemployment rates vary considerable across age-groups (A3) and with worker characteristics such as skill levels. High incidences of long-term unemployment (*e.g.* in Belgium and Italy) raises particular concerns on **labour market attachment** and social distress, and the associated risk is particularly high for older workers, foreign workers or workers belonging to minority groups and low-skilled workers – and frequently these characteristics overlap. Social programme design also affects labour market attachment. Disability and early retirement programmes have been used by workers in some countries (*e.g.* the Netherlands, Poland, Sweden and the UK) to withdraw from the labour market thereby shifting the unemployed to outside the labour force. More recently social programme design in OECD countries is more focussed on increasing labour market participation of (older) workers and making work pay (A6, A12).

Status indicators: Employment (A1), Jobless youth (A3), Jobless households (A4), Retirement ages (A6).
Response indicators: Activation policies (A7), Replacement rates (A12), Tax wedge (A13), Minimum wages (B5), Public social expenditure (B6), Benefit recipiency (B9).

A2. UNEMPLOYMENT

Chart A2.1. Evolution of the unemployment rate for selected countries, 1980-1999

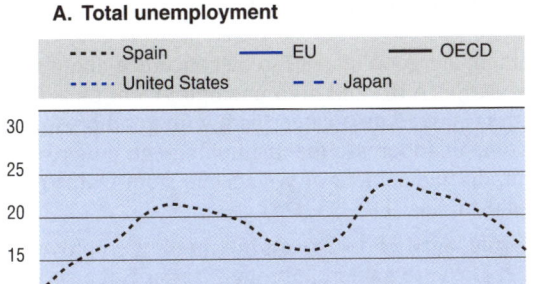

A. Total unemployment

B. Female unemployment

Legend: Spain, EU, OECD, United States, Japan

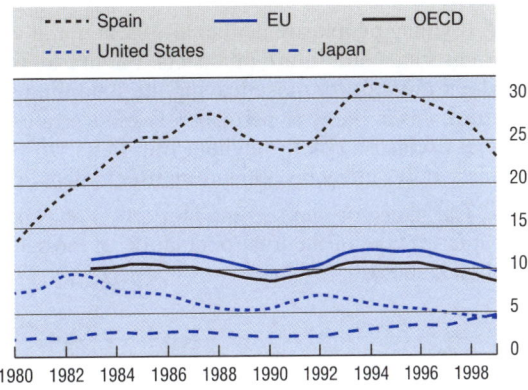

Table A2.1. Unemployment indicators, 1999

	\multicolumn{4}{c	}{Unemployment As a percentage of the labour force}			\multicolumn{3}{c}{Incidence of long-term unemployment As a percentage of unemployment}		
	\multicolumn{4}{c	}{By age groups}	Men	Women	Total	Men	Women
	All ages	15-24	25-54	55-64					
Australia	7.3	13.9	5.7	5.6	7.5	7.2	29.4	31.8	25.8
Austria	4.7	5.9	4.5	4.8	4.7	4.8	31.7	28.1	36.1
Belgium	8.7	22.6	7.4	5.7	7.5	10.3	60.5	60.1	60.9
Canada	7.6	14.0	6.4	5.9	7.9	7.3	11.6	12.8	10.2
Czech Republic	8.7	17.0	7.5	4.8	7.3	10.5	37.1	32.7	40.9
Denmark	5.2	10.0	4.3	4.2	4.5	5.9	20.5	20.9	20.1
Finland	10.3	21.5	8.4	10.2	9.8	10.8	29.6	33.1	26.2
France	11.8	26.6	10.7	8.7	10.3	13.7	40.3	39.0	41.6
Germany	8.7	8.5	7.9	13.9	8.3	9.3	51.7	49.9	54.0
Greece	11.0	29.7	9.0	3.2	7.2	16.8	54.9	44.7	61.5
Hungary	7.0	12.4	6.2	2.7	7.5	6.3	49.5	50.6	47.9
Iceland	1.9	4.4	1.4	1.4	1.4	2.5	11.7	6.6	15.2
Ireland	5.8	8.5	5.3	4.2	6.1	5.5	57.0	63.3	46.9
Italy	11.8	32.9	9.5	4.9	9.0	16.4	61.4	62.1	60.7
Japan	4.9	9.3	4.0	5.4	5.0	4.7	22.4	27.4	14.8
Korea	6.5	14.2	5.8	4.5	7.3	5.3	3.8	4.7	1.9
Luxembourg	2.4	6.8	2.0	1.0	1.7	3.3			
Mexico	2.1	3.4	1.8	0.8	1.8	2.7	1.7	2.7	0.4
Netherlands	3.6	7.4	3.0	2.7	2.7	4.9	43.5	47.7	40.4
New Zealand	6.9	13.7	5.4	5.0	7.1	6.6	20.8	23	17.9
Norway	3.2	9.6	2.4	1.1	3.4	3.0	6.8	7.3	6.3
Poland	10.9	23.2	9.5	5.9	9.5	12.6	37.4	32.5	41.8
Portugal	4.6	8.7	4.0	3.1	4.0	5.3	41.2	39.5	42.9
Spain	15.9	28.5	13.9	9.9	11.1	23.2	51.3	45.4	55.5
Sweden	7.1	14.2	6.2	6.6	7.5	6.7	33.5	36.3	30.1
Switzerland	3.1	5.6	2.6	2.6	2.7	3.6	39.8	40.7	39.0
Turkey	7.7	14.6	6.0	1.9	8.0	6.9	33.7	29.8	44.1
United Kingdom	6.1	12.3	4.9	5.1	6.8	5.1	29.8	34.8	21.6
United States	4.3	9.9	3.2	2.7	4.1	4.4	6.8	7.4	6.2
EU	9.3	17.2	8.1	8.6	8.2	10.9	47.5	46.2	30.3
OECD	**6.4**	**11.8**	**5.4**	**5.2**	**6.0**	**6.9**	**31.2**	**30.3**	**26.4**

Source: OECD (2000), *Employment Outlook*.

Further reading

■ OECD (2000), *Employment Outlook*, Paris. ■ OECD (2000), *Labour Force Statistics*, Paris. ■ OECD (2000), *Pushing Ahead with Reform in Korea, Labour Market and Social Safety-net Policies*, Paris. ■ OECD (1999), *Implementing the OECD Jobs Strategy: Assessing Performance and Policy*, Paris.

© OECD 2001

A3. JOBLESS YOUTH

Definition and measurement

If young people are neither at school nor at work there are good reasons to be concerned about their current status and future prospects. Failure to acquire skills (A10) and high unemployment rates (A2) make it difficult for those leaving the schooling system to move into a career path with good prospects. In turn, this is likely to permanently reduce future income and increase the unemployment, poverty and social exclusion risk throughout life. In its worst form, disengagement of youngsters from mainstream society raises concerns about drug use, violent crime and suicide (D2, D3, D4).

The indicator presents the proportion of young people, aged 15 to 24, not in school or employment as a percentage of the total population of the same age. Data are gathered through labour force surveys (OECD, 2000).

Evidence and explanations

The **policy response** to the prevalence of young people not being in school or work among youth has been different across countries. Some have increased the flexibility of youth labour markets. Others have stressed early and effective measures to ensure that the transition from formal schooling to work is as quick and painless as possible. Others, conversely, have focused on increasing participation in schooling, and/or active labour market programmes (A7). There is considerable difference across countries in the extent with which education systems result in young people being in school until a later age. For example, in 1998, the proportion of 19-year-olds in education only exceeded 60% in the Flemish community of Belgium, France, Germany, Greece, Iceland, the Netherlands and Switzerland (OECD, 2000).

The proportion of youth neither in school or work has diminished since the mid-1980s in the majority of countries for which data are available. This almost universal trend decline was most pronounced for women, the most notable exception being young adult Italian men (Chart A3.1 – trends for 15- to 19-year-olds are fairly similar, see the annex on Internet). One of the underlying reasons is that young people currently spend **more time in education** than they did a decade ago.

The proportion of young people who are neither employed at school or in training is much higher for women than for men and increases at each age (Chart A3.2). Despite the recent **gender gap** reduction (see above), 30% or more of young women in the Czech Republic, Greece, Italy and Turkey are neither in school nor in employment. In contrast, the school to work transition seems relatively smooth in the Netherlands: a mere 2% of those aged 15 to 19 is not in school in or employment.

Status indicators: Unemployment (A2), Drug use and related deaths (D2), Suicide (D3), Crime (D4).
Response indicators: Activation policies (A7), Educational attainment (A10).

A3. JOBLESS YOUTH

Chart A3.1. Evolution of youth joblessness (20-24 years) by gender, mid-1980s to 1998
Percentage point change since mid-1980s

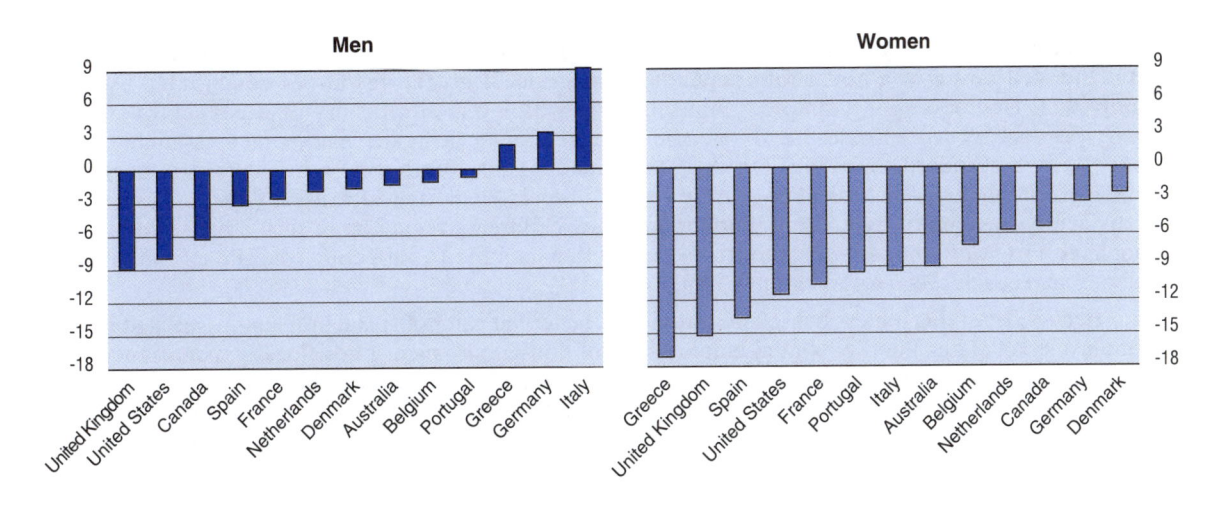

Chart A3.2. Proportion of young people not in school or employment by age group and gender, 1998

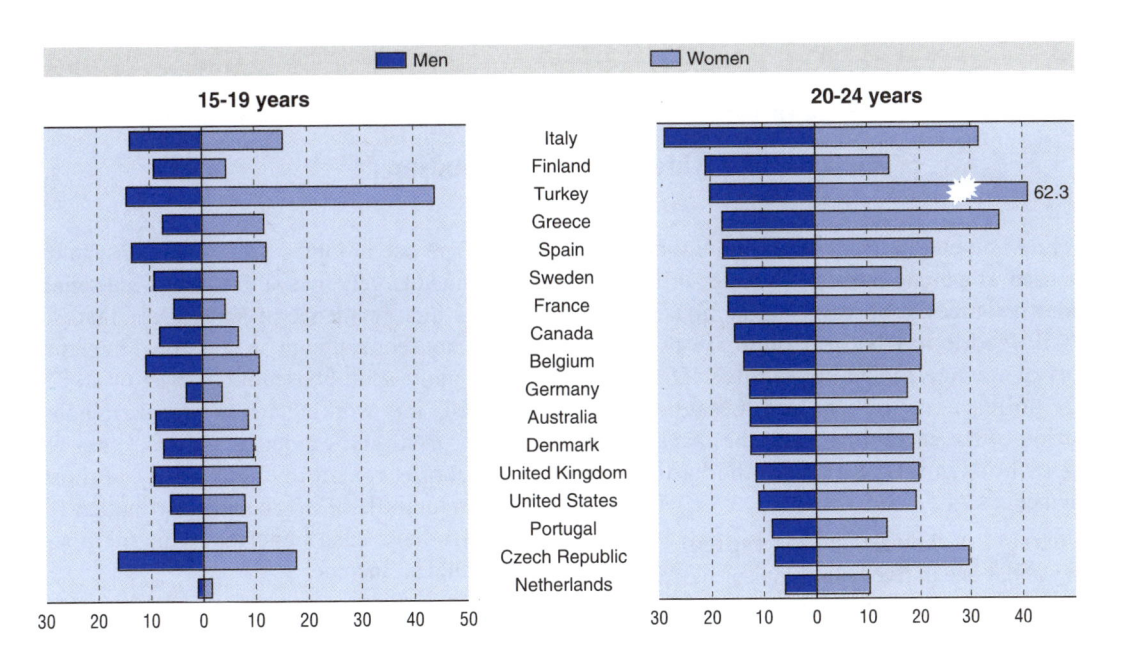

Source: OECD (2000).

Further reading

- OECD (2000), *Education at a Glance – OECD Indicators*, Paris. ■ OECD (1999), *A Caring World: The New Social Policy Agenda*, Paris. ■ OECD (1998), *Family, Market and Community, Equity and Efficiency in Social Policy*, Paris.

A4. JOBLESS HOUSEHOLDS

Definition and measurement

Indicators on employment and unemployment are measures of what individuals do, or do not do. But the well-being of a household depends on the sum of all the resources contributed by its individual members. For example, a household in which one adult individual concentrates on activities such as care of other family members whilst another generates market income might well have a high standard of living. On the other hand, if no member of a household is in paid employment, the household is likely to rely on public social benefits which usually do not support a satisfactory standard of living (B1). Furthermore, any children growing up in such a household may not have a working adult as a role model – a factor often identified as affecting educational and future labour market achievements of children (A9).

Hence, identifying jobless households provides a better indicator of social problems associated with labour market status than individual employment or non-employment rates. Ideally, persistence of household joblessness would be considered, but such information is not available on a comprehensive basis. Of course, not all jobless households are so involuntarily. Retired people may well have generated sufficient income resources to support themselves without working. Therefore the indicator focuses on households with at least one person of working age (15-64) where no member of the household is in employment (part-time or full-time). The charts on jobless households present the risk of non-employment among households of working age, which is given by the proportion of people (non-employed households, then non-employed households with children) to the whole considered population (households, then households with children).

Evidence and explanations

While non-employment at an individual level can be used as a broad measure of under-utilisation of labour resources, joblessness at the households' level will lead to **hardship** if there are no other sources of income in the households. Different welfare policies may be required if a substantial proportion of the unemployed and the inactive are living in households with no other adults in employment (A7).

Chart A4.1 shows that in a **typical OECD country** about one in five households of working age has no employment income of any sort, ranging from a low of just over 5% in Mexico to a high of over 27% in Finland. This proportion has risen in 12 of the 15 countries where information is available from the mid-1980s, with particularly sharp increases in New Zealand, Belgium, Italy and France. On the other hand, in both the Netherlands and Denmark the proportion of jobless households has fallen (see the annex on Internet).

The rise in joblessness at the household level is explained largely by a shift towards **household types** with a high incidence of joblessness, that is, single-adult households, with an additional impetus arising from multi-adult households (Chart A4.2) becoming "sorted" into working and non-working households. Unsurprisingly, evidence suggests that workless households constitute the majority of those in the bottom quintile of the income distribution (B2), and usually have cash benefits as the main source of households' income.

Status indicators: Employment (A1), Unemployment (A2), Relative poverty (B1), Income inequality (B2).
Response indicators: Activation policies (A7), Early childhood education and care (A9), Public social expenditure (B6).

A4. JOBLESS HOUSEHOLDS

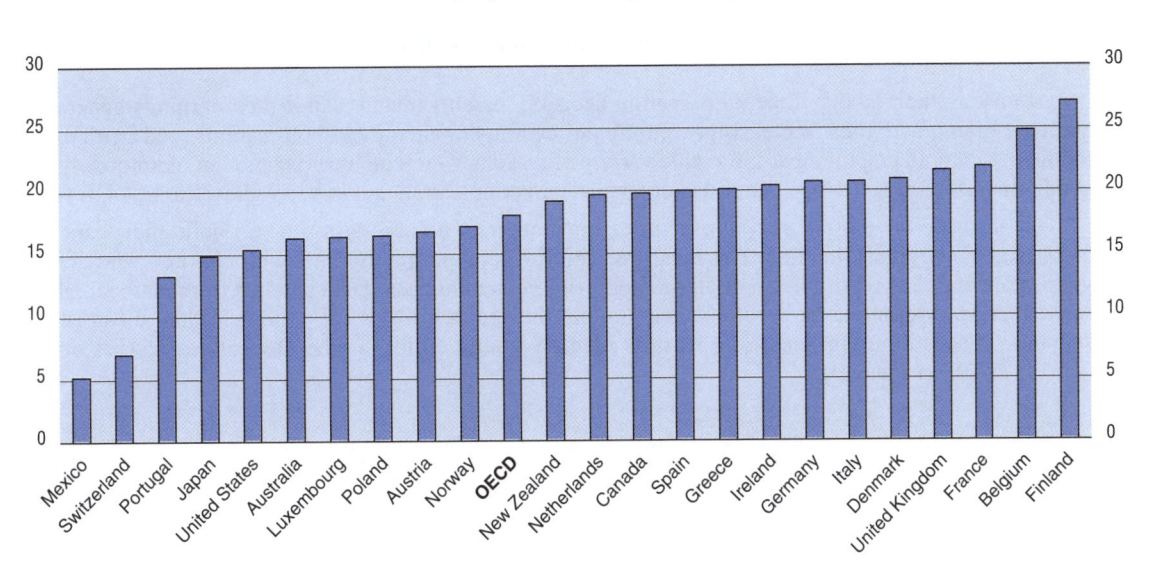

Chart A4.1. **Rate of non-employment among working age households, 1996**

Chart A4.2. **Rate of non-employment for working-age households with children, 1996**

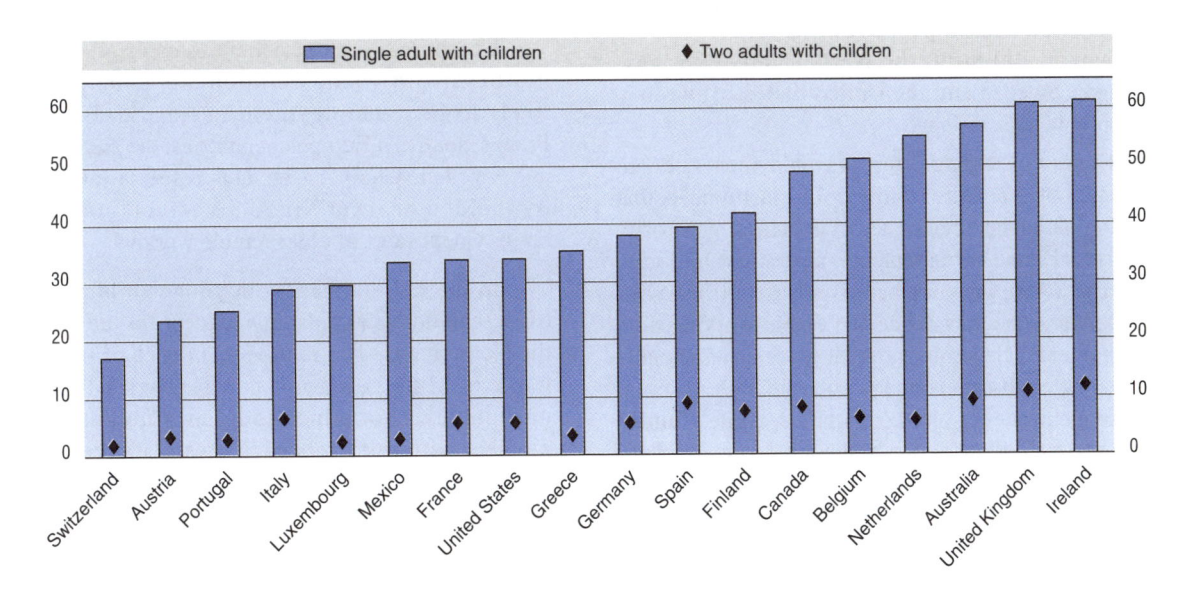

Source: OECD (1998).

Further reading

■ Gregg, P. and J. Wadsworth, (1999), "Mind the gap, please. The changing nature of entry jobs in Britain", LSE Centre for Economic Performance Working Paper, No. 796, London. ■ Gregg, P. and J. Wadsworth, (1996), "It takes two: Employment polarisation in the OECD", LSE Centre for Economic Performance Working Paper, No. 304, London. ■ OECD (1998), *Employment Outlook*, Paris.

A5. WORKING MOTHERS

Definition and measurement

In making their labour force participation decision, parents must balance their earnings-generating and care-giving activities. Increasingly, public policy aims to encourage both parents, and particularly mothers, to stay in employment for a wide variety of reasons which include: promotion of autonomy and gender mainstreaming (B4), a better use of labour market potential, and poverty alleviation (A4, B1).

To illustrate the labour market outcomes for mothers who are trying to reconcile their care and employment activities, this indicator measures employment among mothers with children who are not yet 6 years of age as a proportion of all mothers with young children. Data is taken from national labour force surveys. Measurement problems exist in that the age thresholds for young children differ across surveys. For example, in Australia, records identify young children who are not yet 5 years of age (see the annex on Internet).

Evidence and explanations

Employment rates of women (A1) and of mothers with young children have increased in almost all countries over the last ten years (Chart A5.1). In 1999, **maternal employment rates** exceeded 60% in Austria, Belgium, the Netherlands, Norway, Portugal, Sweden and the United States, while they were below 40% in Japan.

High or increasing maternal employment rates are facilitated by a mixture of four policy instruments that vary in relative importance across countries: generosity of parental leave arrangements, access to child-care facilities (A9), in-work benefits for families with children, and the prevalence of flexible working time arrangements. Generous parental leave arrangements and public child-care supports underlie high maternal employment rates in Nordic countries, while "**family work reconciliation**" in the Netherlands is more likely to be achieved through flexible working time arrangements and part-time employment (Table A5.2), although child care capacity has grown rapidly in recent years. Strong direct financial incentives to work (A12) and widespread use of (informal) care arrangements underlie high maternal employment rates in the US.

There is a difference between "**being employed**" (which includes those on leave, including maternity leave) and "**being in work**" (which does not), and this discrepancy varies with the generosity of leave arrangements and is thus relatively high in Austria, France, Germany and the Nordic countries (Table A5.1).

Compared to employment rates of all women, **mothers** with young children are actually more likely to be in **employment** in Austria, Belgium, France, southern European countries, the Netherlands and Sweden (Chart A5.1). This result is influenced by "added-worker" income effects and low employment rates of older female workers.

In the EU, mothers with young children more often than not work full-time, except for the UK and the Netherlands. The relative incidence of part-time work is highest among mothers with low and medium levels of **educational attainment** (A10): mothers with relatively high levels of educational attainment are more likely to be in full-time employment.

Status indicators: Employment (A1), Jobless households (A4), Relative poverty (B1), Gender wage gap (B4).
Response indicators: Early childhood education and care (A9), Educational attainment (A10), Replacement rates (A12).

A5. WORKING MOTHERS

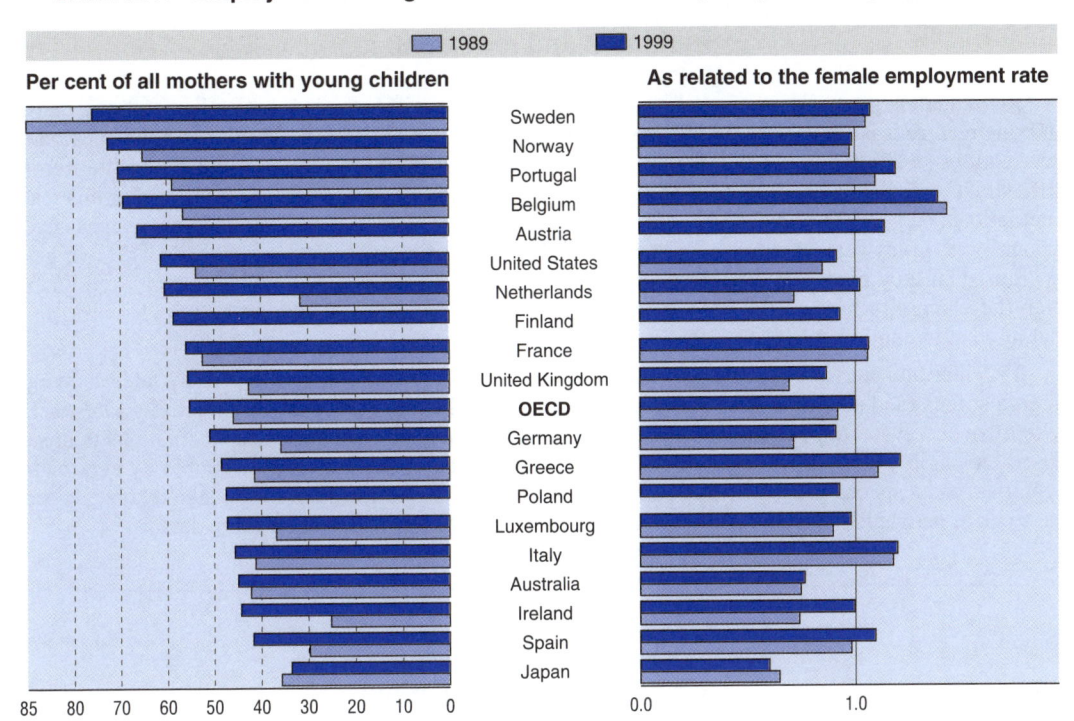

Chart A5.1. **Employment among mothers with a child not yet 6 years of age, 1989-1999**

Per cent of all mothers with young children — *As related to the female employment rate*

(Countries listed: Sweden, Norway, Portugal, Belgium, Austria, United States, Netherlands, Finland, France, United Kingdom, **OECD**, Germany, Greece, Poland, Luxembourg, Italy, Australia, Ireland, Spain, Japan)

Table A5.1. **Employment and being in work for mothers with a child not yet 6 years of age, 1999**

	Employment rate	Proportion of employed mothers using parental leave during the survey week
Austria	66.5	5.3
Belgium	69.5	1.5
Denmark		3.0
Finland	58.8	2.3
France	56.2	2.0
Germany	51.1	3.6
Greece	48.6	0.4
Iceland		2.3
Ireland	44.4	1.5
Italy	45.7	2.0
Netherlands	60.7	0.6
Norway		4.6
Portugal	70.6	0.7
Spain	41.8	0.9
Sweden		2.9
United Kingdom	55.8	1.2

Table A5.2. **Proportion of part-time employment in total female employment, 1997**

	Mothers with a child not yet 6 years of age, by level of educational attainment			All women
	High	Medium	Low	
Austria	36	45	37	21
Belgium	34	41	47	32
Denmark				
Finland	7	16	13	13
France	32	39	42	25
Germany	45	66	44	31
Greece	7	9	13	14
Iceland				
Ireland	16	28	48	27
Italy	15	18	22	22
Netherlands	89	90	89	55
Norway				
Portugal	2	5	13	17
Spain	12	19	26	17
Sweden				
United Kingdom	55	70	63	41

Sources: National labour force surveys (see the annex on Internet).

Further reading

- Adema, W. (2001, forthcoming), "An overview of benefits that foster the reconciliation of work and family life in OECD countries", Labour Market and Social Policy Occasional Paper, Paris. ■ Evans, J.M. (2001), "Firms' contribution to the reconciliation between work and family life", Labour Market and Social Policy Occasional Paper, No. 48, Paris. ■ OECD (1999), *A Caring World: The New Social Policy Agenda*, Paris. ■ OECD (1998), *Family, Market and Community, Equity and Efficiency in Social Policy*, Paris.

A6. RETIREMENT AGES

Definition and measurement

Retirement is generally associated with cessation of work from a "main" job and receipt of a pension, and one recurrent issue in pension system reform concerns the age of retirement, and relevant financial implications (A13). However, trends in retirement ages are difficult to measure directly, as "retirement" differs in its meaning across countries and between pension arrangements within countries. For this reason, international comparisons have to use comparisons of movements out of the labour force, as measured by labour force survey data, as a proxy for "retirement". Those above a specified age (usually 45) are regarded as "retired" if they are not in the labour force at the time of the survey). Net movement into retirement is then the change in time in the proportion of the population above 45 which is neither working nor classified as unemployed.

This indicator measures net withdrawal from the labour force by comparing activity rates at five year intervals: thus the latest figure for most countries is derived from a comparison of activity rates in 1999 with those in 1994. They are therefore a less accurate indicator of business cycle fluctuations than series based on single year data would be. For ages above 65, activity rates are not available by age for most countries, and a special procedure has been used to estimate "flow" rates out of the labour force, based on the stock of people in the labour force aged 65 and over. See Scherer (2001) for more details.

Evidence and explanations

Overall labour force withdrawal should be considered in the context of interacting factors whose importance varies across countries and time. These factors include: business cycle trends underlying labour demand (A1), demographic trends and the maturing of populations covered by pension plans and their generosity (B6, B7, B9). For the few countries for which data are available from 1960 onwards, "retirement" ages are lower now than in 1960 (Chart A6.1), but **trends** vary considerably. Trends in "retirement" ages in Japan and the United States seem far more susceptible to cyclical fluctuations than in France, where pension arrangements facilitated a reduction in "retirement" ages from 1965 to the late 1970s. For the 1983-1999 period, there is no evidence of any general tendency to retire from the labour force earlier or later: retirement ages rose in eight countries and fell in eight for men, and rose in six but fell in nine for women (Chart A6.2).

Average "retirement" ages for men range from 59 (France, Italy) to 69 (Japan), with an average **across OECD countries** of 62, with similar results for women. Many women enter the labour force after the age of 45, so net withdrawal only starts after age 50 or 55. For countries where men do not start to withdraw until 55 either (such as Japan), this makes no difference to the results, but in most countries men start to retire relatively early. The apparent similarity in "retirement" ages between men and women is in part the result of this factor.

Status indicators: Employment (A1).
Response indicators: Tax wedge (A13), Public social expenditure (B6), Private social expenditure (B7), Benefit recipiency (B9).

A6. RETIREMENT AGES

Chart A6.1. **Average age of "retirement" for selected countries since 1960**

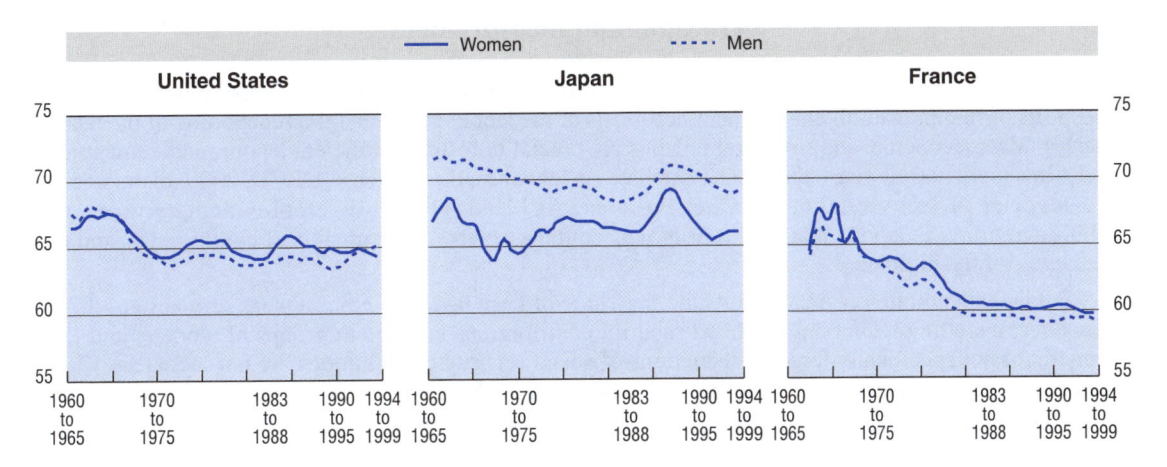

Chart A6.2. **Average age of withdrawal from the labour force since 1983**

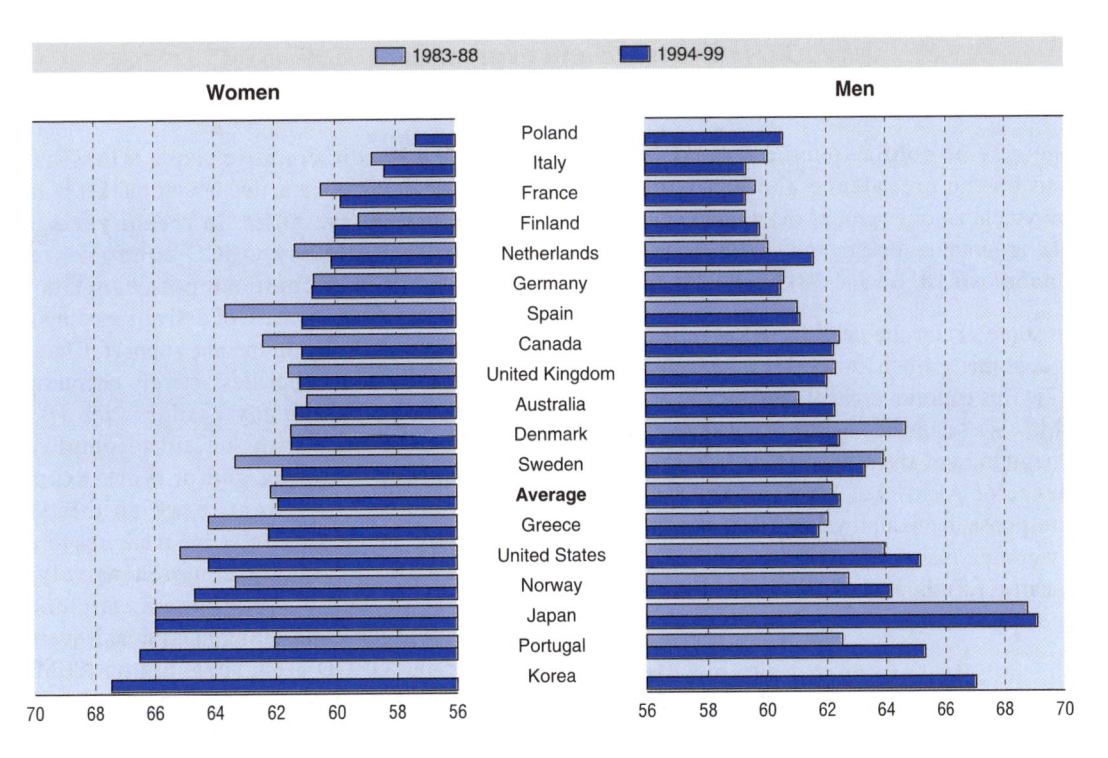

Source: Scherer (2001).

Further reading

- Scherer, P. (2001), "Age of withdrawal from the labour market in OECD countries", Labour Market and Social Policy Occasional Papers, No. 49, Paris. ■ OECD (2000), *Reforms for an Ageing Society*, Paris. ■ OECD (1998), *Maintaining Prosperity in an Ageing Society*, Paris. ■ OECD (1995), *The Transition from Work to Retirement*, Paris.

A7. ACTIVATION POLICIES

Definition and measurement

Activation policies comprise a range of public measures intended to improve beneficiaries' prospects of finding gainful employment, job-skills of the labour force, and the functioning of the labour market. Macroeconomic and structural policies are crucial in fostering efficient labour market outcomes (A1). In a more narrow sense the OECD database on labour market policies (OECD, 2000) distinguishes 5 categories of Active Labour Market Policies (ALMPs): (1) public employment services and administration, (2) labour market training, (3) youth measures, (4) subsidised employment and (5) measures for the disabled.

Public expenditure on ALMPs include the value of cash benefits, employment services and fiscal measures, including reductions of social security contributions targeted at groups of workers and jobs (general or not specifically targeted reductions of social security contributions are not included). There are measurement problems: for example, spending on ALMPs by lower tiers of government is not comprehensively recorded for all countries, *e.g.* Canada and Switzerland.

Evidence and explanations

The size of public spending on ALMPs is affected by the prevalence and persistence of unemployment among (groups of) workers (A3, A4, and B9), programme design and administration, and policy priorities (A8, B6 and B8).

To some extent the need for ALMPs increases when economic growth slows down and *vice versa* (A1, A2). This **counter-cyclical tendency** in spending on ALMPs is exemplified by the Swedish experience in the beginning of the 1990s (Chart A7.1). As the prevalence of ALMPs at least in part, reflects a policy response to unemployment fluctuations, cross-country comparison of ALMP-spending in a given year (Chart A7.2) should be considered in the light of the stage of each country in the business cycle.

The largest **components of spending** on ALMPs constitute training, subsidized employment and the provision of job search counselling and the administration of employment services. Spending on ALMPs varies with the type of intervention: direct job creation is more expensive per client than intensive job-search counselling, while it is not necessarily more effective in enhancing long-term employment and earnings potential of the individual. Hence, relatively low spending on ALMPs does not necessarily reflect badly on a country, as it may evidence high economic activity levels and cost-effective programme design.

The Nordic countries have a long-standing tradition of pursuing active labour market policies on a comprehensive basis. In recent years, public authorities in many OECD countries reduced generosity of income support benefits which contributed to an increase of **active** spending relative to **passive** spending on income support (Chart A7.2). Simultaneously, authorities actively encouraged the unemployed to take any available job (B3, B5), where necessary with the aid of employment-counselling, training and/or work-experience placements. The extent to which this shift in emphasis from passive to active measures took place is difficult to evidence comprehensively in the absence of data on programme efficiency and intensity of job-counselling measures. Nevertheless, across the OECD area, spending on ALMPs has remained fairly stable since 1996, while unemployment fell by 1.6 percentage points over the same period which also contributed to a decline in passive spending on income support.

Status indicators: Employment (A1), Unemployment (A2), Jobless youth (A3), Jobless households (A4), Relative poverty (B1), Low paid employment (B3). **Response indicators**: Spending on education (A8), Replacement rates (A12), Minimum wages (B5), Public social expenditure (B6), Benefit recipiency (B9).

A7. ACTIVATION POLICIES

Chart A7.1. **Active labour market public spending, 1985-1999**

····· Sweden — EU — OECD – – United States ····· Japan

A. Per cent of GDP

B. Per cent of total LMP spending

Chart A7.2. **Active and passive labour market public spending, 1999 (per cent of GDP)**

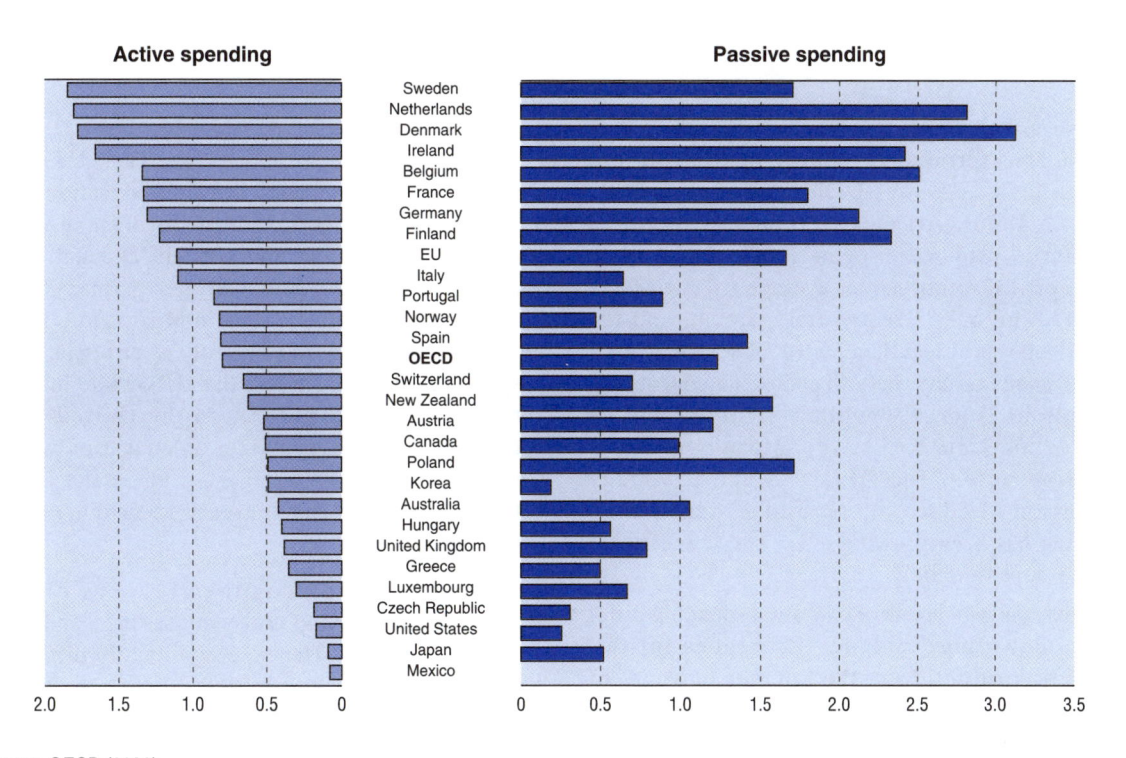

Active spending — Passive spending

Sweden, Netherlands, Denmark, Ireland, Belgium, France, Germany, Finland, EU, Italy, Portugal, Norway, Spain, **OECD**, Switzerland, New Zealand, Austria, Canada, Poland, Korea, Australia, Hungary, United Kingdom, Greece, Luxembourg, Czech Republic, United States, Japan, Mexico

Source: OECD (2000).

Further reading

- Fay, R. (1997), "Enhancing the effectiveness of active labour market policies: evidence from programme evaluations in OECD countries", *Labour Market and Social Policy Occasional Papers*, No. 18, OECD, Paris. ■ Martin, J.P. (2000), "What works among active labour market policies: evidence from OECD countries experiences", *OECD Economic Studies*, No. 30, 2000/1, Paris. ■ OECD (2000), *Employment Outlook*, Paris.

© OECD 2001

49

A8. SPENDING ON EDUCATION

Definition and measurement

Education plays a role in providing individuals with the knowledge, skills and competencies to participate more effectively in society. Spending on education relative to GDP thus gives a measure of how much a country invests in human capital. The indicator focuses on total (public and private) expenditure on educational institutions, including public subsidies to private institutions and households insofar as these translate into payments to educational institutions. Data on spending on educational institutions do not include: other public spending on education (*e.g.* subsidies for student living costs or favourable tax treatment of households with children in education), and other direct private spending on education (*e.g.* costs for textbooks or transport).

Cross-country comparisons of education expenditure per student are based on purchasing power parities, and not market exchange rates. PPPs reflect the amount of a national currency that will buy the same basket of goods and services in a given country as the US dollar in the United States. Comprehensive information on PPPs regarding the cost of education alone is not available.

Evidence and explanations

For almost all OECD countries for which data are available, **spending on educational institutions** grew at least as fast as GDP from 1990 to 1997 (OECD, 2000). All OECD countries devote a substantial proportion of national resources to educational institutions: on average 6.1% of GDP in 1997, and only Greece, Italy, Japan, and the Netherlands spent less than 5% of GDP (Chart A8.1 and the annex on Internet). Spending on educational institutions is largely publicly financed and on average amounts to 14% of total government spending across the OECD. Since 1990, the proportion of education spending in all public spending has been growing everywhere except for Finland, Japan and Italy.

Reasons why levels of education spending differ **across countries** include differences in: the population of children, the number of years of compulsory education, participation in non-compulsory education, class sizes, and differences in spending levels per student across different levels of education (Chart A8.2). Indeed, countries have adopted very different policies regarding the distribution of resources among students at different education levels, although in all countries expenditure per student rise sharply with the level of education. On average OECD countries spend US$3 769 per student at the primary level, US$5 507 per student at the secondary level, and US$10 893 per student at the tertiary level of education. These averages mask considerable differences in expenditure per student across OECD countries. For example, in 1997 spending per primary school student varied from US$935 in Mexico to US$6 596 in Denmark, while per a student at tertiary level spending varied from less than US$3 000 in Turkey to more than US$17 000 in the United States. Evidently, overall spending on education will rise faster with growing numbers of university students than when a similar increase in primary school children occurs.

Education predominantly takes place in traditional school and university settings, and is thus **labour intensive**. Hence, cross-country differences in education spending at all levels of education are strongly related to student/staff ratios and teachers' salaries.

Status indicators: Employment (A1), Unemployment (A2), Income inequality (B2).
Response indicators: Early childhood education and care (A9), Educational attainment (A10), Literacy (A11).

A8. SPENDING ON EDUCATION

Chart A8.1. **Expenditure on educational institutions by source of funds, 1997**
Per cent of GDP

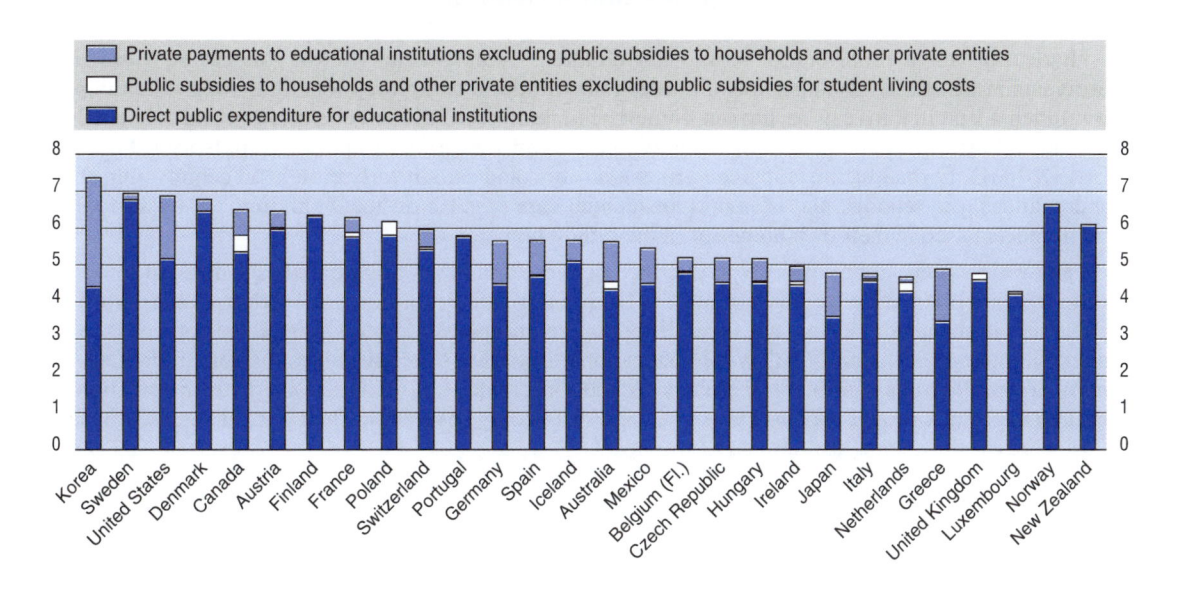

- Private payments to educational institutions excluding public subsidies to households and other private entities
- Public subsidies to households and other private entities excluding public subsidies for student living costs
- Direct public expenditure for educational institutions

Chart A8.2. **Expenditure per student in public and private institutions by level of education, 1997**
(US$ PPPs)

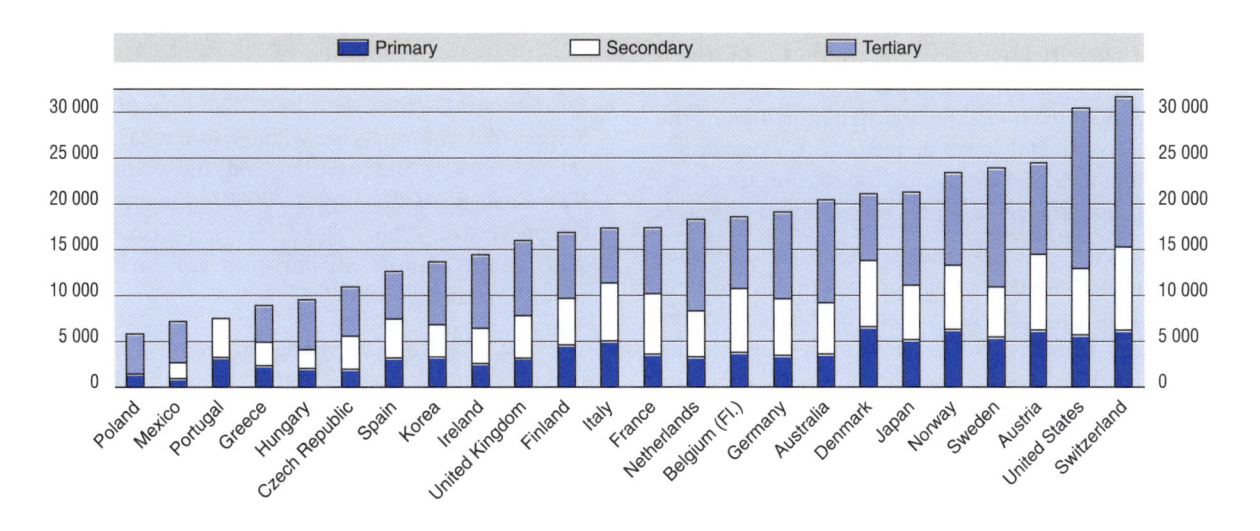

Primary | Secondary | Tertiary

Source: OECD (2000).

Further reading

- OECD (2000), *Education at a Glance – OECD Indicators*, Paris.

A9. EARLY CHILDHOOD EDUCATION AND CARE

Definition and measurement

Parents are the main carers for very young children. Complementary to the role played by parents, relatives, friends and neighbours, social interaction with peers and professionally trained staff can play an important part in the early education of young children. Early childhood education and care (ECEC) includes all arrangements providing care and education for children under compulsory school age (OECD, 2001). Formal facilities include group education and care in early childhood centres (nurseries, kindergartens, pre-schools, play-schools), residential care (*e.g.* for disabled children), or by accredited childminders based in their own homes or in the family home.

The wide variety in provision types, service delivery and hours of care makes it difficult to obtain comparable information across countries. Comparability problems are further exacerbated by differences in mandatory school ages and different age-groupings reported by national sources (see the annex on Internet). Data on ECEC within educational institutions include education for children aged 3 and over, enrolled in pre-primary or primary school programmes (OECD, 2000). Thus information on children in group-care and playgroups as in Chart A9.1 is only covered in Chart A9.2 if such settings are considered as educational institutions.

Evidence and explanations

The **use of ECEC facilities** by parents and young children (up to 7 years of age) depends on a wide range of factors. These include: parental preferences, the presence of a second adult within households, parental labour force attachment, the nature of parental leave benefits (B6), mandatory schooling ages, the availability of both informal and formal care arrangements, the cost of formal services and their quality.

Across countries there are wide differences in the extent to which very young children use formal services (Chart A9.1). Less than 10% of the children 0-3 years in Austria, the Czech republic, Greece, Italy, Korea, the Netherlands, and Spain ever uses formal day care services, while at least 40% of this age group uses formal child-care facilities in Canada, Denmark, New Zealand, Norway, the Slovak Republic, Sweden and the United States. Increased female labour force participation (A1) in many countries has contributed to the rising demand for ECEC facilities which help parents to reconcile their work and care obligations, while the opposite trend has materialised in the Czech republic. With the demise of the communist regime the use of ECEC facilities by 0 to 3-year-olds has fallen dramatically from 20% in 1989 to 1% in 1998 (OECD, 2001).

The proportion of children using formal arrangements rises with **age**. The proportion of 3-years olds in formal care within educational systems exceeds 80% in Belgium, Iceland, Italy, Spain, and New Zealand, and is almost 100% in France with its comprehensive "école maternelle" system (Chart A9.1). At 6 years, almost all children are enrolled in educational institutions.

The proportion of young children using formal services is not always higher in countries with extensive **public** provision (*e.g.* Nordic countries) than in countries where many services are **privately** provided (*e.g.* the United States). However, the cost of formal child-care relative to household income is much higher for average American income earners than for their Danish counterparts.

Status indicators: Employment (A1).
Response Indicators: Spending on education (A8), Public social expenditure (B6).

A9. EARLY CHILDHOOD EDUCATION AND CARE

Chart A9.1. **Proportion of young children who use day care facilities up to mandatory schooling age, 1998/1999**

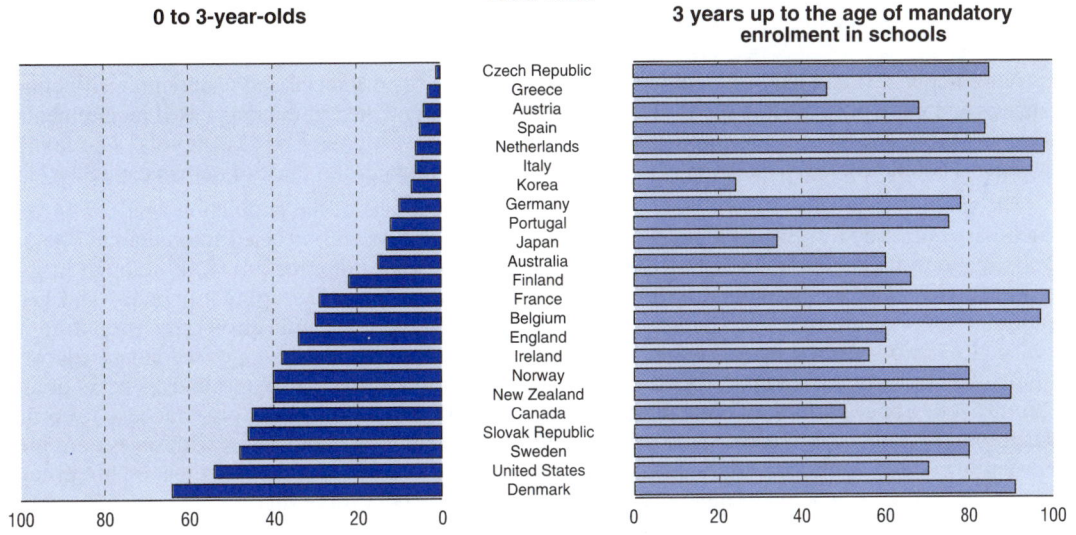

Source: Adema (2001).

Chart A9.2. **Enrolment rates at the ages of 3 and 6 in educational institutions, 1998**

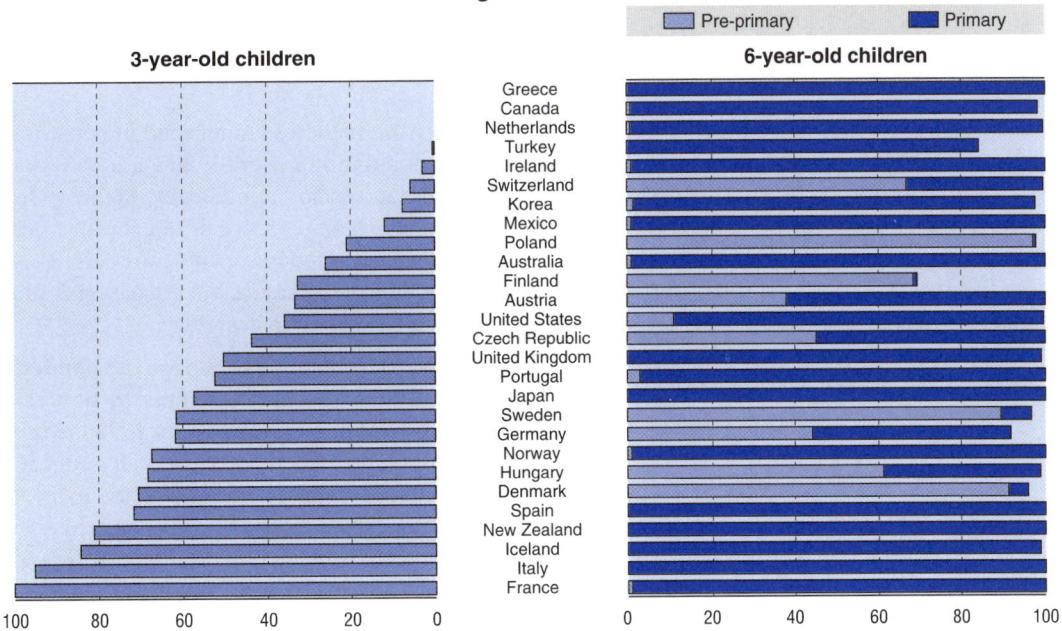

Source: OECD (2000).

Further reading

- Adema, W. (2001, forthcoming), "An overview of benefits that foster the reconciliation of work and family life in OECD countries", Labour Market and Social Policy Occasional Paper, Paris. ■ OECD (2001), *Starting Strong – Early Childhood Education and Care*, Paris. ■ OECD (2000), *Education at a Glance – OECD Indicators*, Paris. ■ Kamerman, S.B. (2000), "Early childhood education and care: An overview of developments in the OECD countries", *International Journal of Educational Research*, 33(1), pp. 7-29. ■ Rostgaard, T. and T. Fridberg (1998), "Caring for children and older people: A comparison of European policies and practices", The Danish National Institute of Social Research, Copenhagen.

A10. EDUCATIONAL ATTAINMENT

Definition and measurement

A well-educated and well-trained population is important for the social and economic well-being of countries and individuals (A1, A2, B1). Technological progress and, hence, the rising skill requirements of labour markets underscore the importance of continuous development of skill levels. The level of educational attainment in a population is the commonly used proxy for the stock of human capital (A11).

The attainment profiles shown here are based on the percentage of the population aged 25-64 years which has completed a specified highest level of education. The recently refined International Standard Classification of Education (ISCED 1997) defines different levels of educational attainment in great detail (OECD, 2000). The indicators here are based on three broad groupings: primary and lower secondary education, upper secondary education and tertiary education: university education and advanced vocation-specific programmes. The distinction between lower and upper secondary education often coincides with the age up to which enrolment in education is mandatory (around 16 years of age). In contrast to upper secondary education, lower secondary education never gives access to tertiary education programmes or advanced vocation-specific programmes. For countries with no system break between lower and upper secondary education, the first three years in secondary education are grouped as lower secondary education. Data are derived from national labour force surveys.

Evidence and explanations

In the majority of OECD countries, more than 60% of the working age population have completed at least upper secondary education, and this proportion is over 80 per cent in Canada, the Czech Republic, Germany, Japan, Norway, Switzerland and the United States (Chart A10.1). In contrast, the educational structure of the adult population shows a rather different profile in Greece, Italy, Mexico, Portugal, Spain and Turkey, where less than 50% of the population aged 25-64 years has completed upper secondary education. Furthermore, less than 10% of the adult population has completed tertiary education in Italy, Portugal and Turkey.

The rising skill requirements of labour markets and higher expectations by individuals and society have inspired a larger proportion of the **young** population to obtain higher qualifications than in the past. Comparing educational attainment of the population aged 25-34 years with that of the age-group 55-64 shows that the proportion of individuals who have completed upper secondary education has increased in all OECD countries (Chart A10.2). This effect is particularly pronounced in countries whose adult population generally has a lower attainment level, as for example in Greece, Mexico, Spain and Turkey. As cross-country differences in educational attainment for younger people are relatively small, cross-country differences in educational attainment levels are expected to decrease.

As for younger age groups the **gender gap** in educational attainment seems to be decreasing (OECD, 2000). Nevertheless, in 1998 the proportion of males who had completed tertiary education was considerably higher than for females in Greece, Germany, Japan, Korea, Mexico, the Netherlands and Switzerland, while in Canada, Finland, New Zealand, Portugal and Sweden, it was the other way around (Chart A10.3).

Status indicators: Employment (A1), Unemployment (A2), Relative poverty (B1).
Response indicators: Spending on education (A8), Literacy (A11).

A10. EDUCATIONAL ATTAINMENT

Chart A10.1. **Distribution of the population 25 to 64 years by level of educational attainment, 1998**

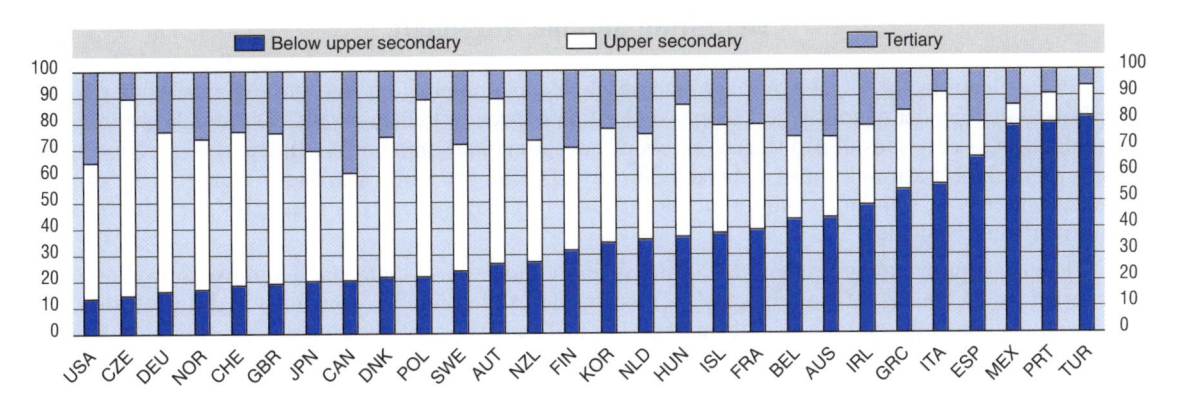

Chart A10.2. **Percentage of the population that has attained at least upper secondary education by age group (1998)**

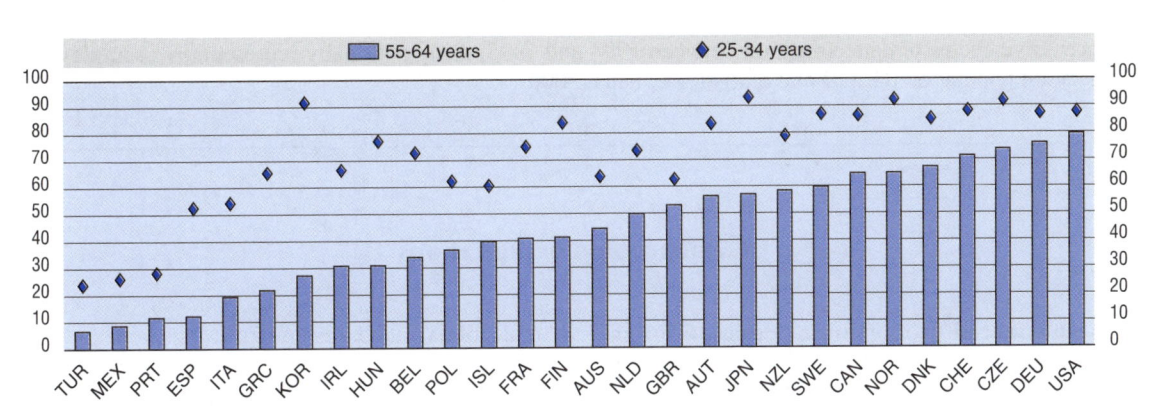

Chart A10.3. **Percentage of the population aged 25-64 that has attained tertiary education by gender (1998)**

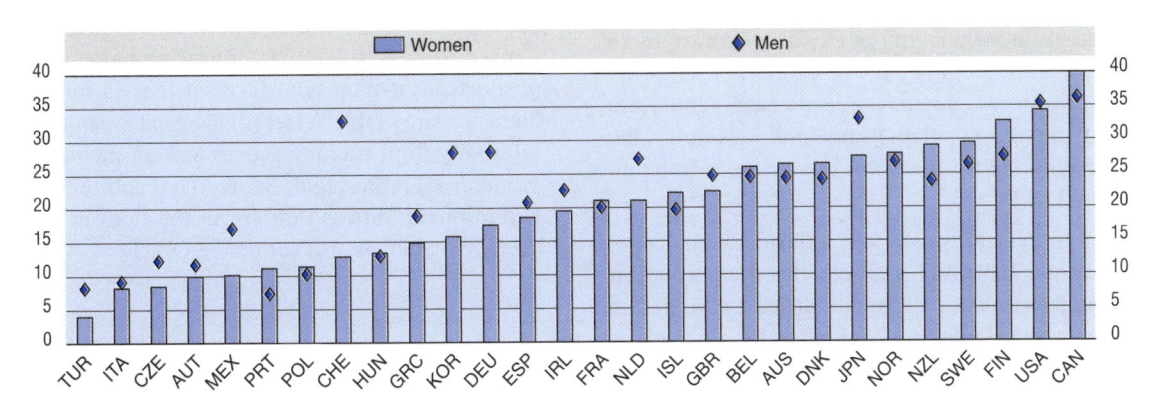

Source: OECD (2000).

Further reading

■ OECD (2000), *Education at a Glance – OECD Indicators*, Paris.

© OECD 2001

A11. LITERACY

Definition and measurement

People learn in school, at work, at home, through social interaction, and through many other daily activities, thereby continuously developing one nation's stock of human capital. The standard approach in measuring skills considers different levels of educational attainment (A10). But the more recently developed International Adult Literacy Survey (IALS) provides a broader framework for the measurement of skills and competencies of adult populations for the countries for which such information is available.

The concept of literacy covers the ability of individuals to: 1) understand and use information in general text documents – "prose literacy"; 2) locate and use information contained in different formats, *e.g.* application forms and maps – "document literacy"; and 3), apply arithmetic operations. Although literacy scores vary across these three groupings, indicators presented here concern the commonly used "document literacy" scores for the proportion of the population aged 16 to 65. IALS literacy score-levels 1 and 2 are considered "low", while levels 4 and 5 are "high"; IALS literacy score-level 3 or "moderate" is considered to be a suitable minimum for coping with the demands of everyday life and work in a complex, advanced society. Not surprisingly, the risk of being in unemployment (A2) and/or having a low-income (B1, B3) is higher for someone with low literacy proficiency. The data presented here were collected by the countries participating in the International Adult Literacy Survey in successive cycles of data collection between 1994 and 1998, using nationally representative samples of the adult population (OECD and Statistics Canada, 2000).

Evidence and explanations

A substantial proportion of populations in OECD countries has low literacy scores. In fact, about 40% of populations in most **OECD countries** have literacy scores that are considered to be below the level necessary for coping with everyday life in a complex and advanced societies, and in Poland and Portugal, this concerns three quarters of the population. In the majority of OECD countries, more than half of the adult population scores at least at the moderate literacy level, while literacy scores are highest amongst populations in Nordic countries, the Netherlands and the Flemish Community in Belgium (Chart A11.1).

Literacy scores also vary considerably across **age groups**. Table A11.1 reveals that the proportion of younger adults (26-35) with at least a moderate literacy is often three times as high as for older adults (age 56-65). Compared to those who were at school 40 years ago, younger adults generally have been longer in formal education attaining higher educational standards (A10). It thus appears that the positive effect of recently completed formal education at higher levels on literacy scores is much stronger than positive effects generated by relatively long life-experience.

Gender differences in literacy scores do exist but seem relatively small. Except for Canada and the United States, all OECD countries have a larger proportion of men who have at least a moderate literacy score (Table A11.1). This gender gap towards relatively high literacy scores among men is most pronounced in Portugal, Switzerland and the United Kingdom: countries that are in the bottom half of average literacy scores across the OECD.

Status indicators: Unemployment (A2), Relative poverty (B1), Low paid employment (B3).
Response indicators: Educational attainment (A10).

A11. LITERACY

Chart A11.1. **Adult population by level of document literacy, 1998**
Unit: % of people scoring this level

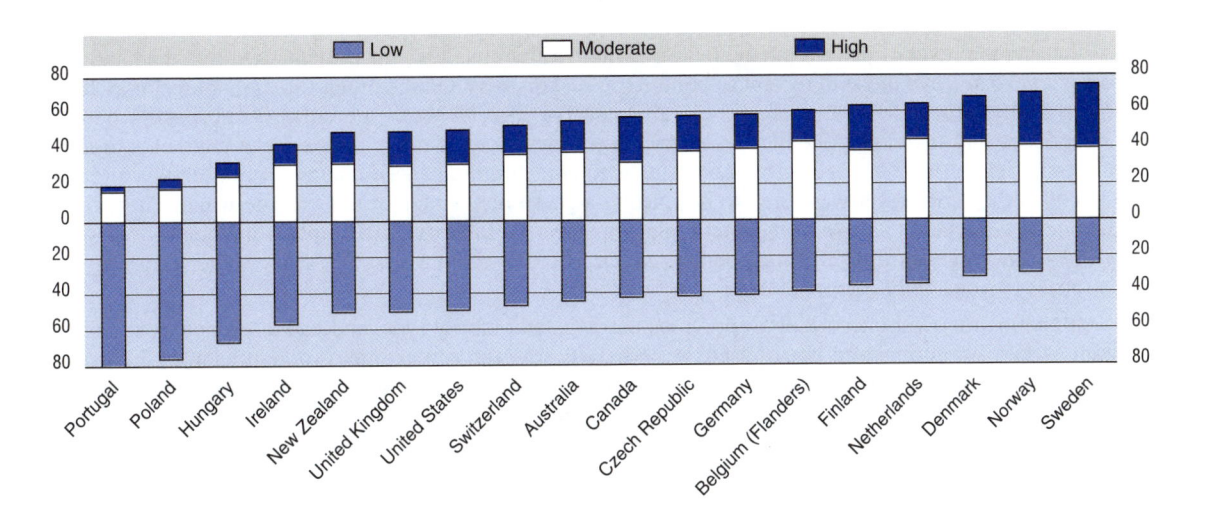

[Stacked bar chart showing Low, Moderate, High literacy levels for: Portugal, Poland, Hungary, Ireland, New Zealand, United Kingdom, United States, Switzerland, Australia, Canada, Czech Republic, Germany, Belgium (Flanders), Finland, Netherlands, Denmark, Norway, Sweden]

Table A11.1. **Distribution of the population with at least moderate literacy scores by age and gender, 1998**
As a percentage of the population with at least moderate literacy scores

	By age					By sex	
	16-25	26-35	36-45	46-55	56-65	Men	Women
Portugal	46.3	21.5	16.1	10.9	5.1	55.7	44.3
Poland	32.1	26.3	25.3	11.0	5.3	52.3	47.7
Hungary	31.9	25.0	21.7	15.9	5.4	51.0	49.0
Ireland	31.8	25.0	23.1	13.0	7.1	53.4	46.6
New Zealand	24.2	26.5	25.1	16.4	7.8	50.3	49.7
United Kingdom	22.4	25.9	25.3	17.7	8.7	55.4	44.6
United States	15.6	25.1	27.9	20.1	11.4	46.4	53.6
Switzerland	21.9	31.0	20.1	17.1	9.9	54.6	45.4
Australia	25.2	26.0	25.3	16.2	7.4	52.2	47.8
Canada	23.1	28.9	27.1	14.2	6.6	49.5	50.5
Czech Republic	26.6	18.4	23.3	22.1	9.6	52.7	47.3
Germany	19.4	27.5	20.7	19.4	13.0	52.3	47.7
Belgium (Flanders)	25.1	28.4	22.8	16.3	7.4	53.3	46.7
Finland	24.6	26.3	24.1	18.4	6.6	50.3	49.7
Netherlands	25.4	28.6	23.2	15.3	7.6	53.7	46.3
Denmark	21.2	26.8	22.6	19.4	10.0	53.8	46.2
Norway	21.9	28.1	25.4	17.6	7.0	53.4	46.6
Sweden	23.8	23.9	22.3	18.7	11.4	51.9	48.1

Source: OECD and Statistics Canada (2000).

Further reading

■ OECD and Statistics Canada (2000), *Literacy in the Information Age: Final Report of the International Adult Literacy Survey*, Paris/Ottawa. ■ OECD (2000), *Education at a Glance – OECD Indicators*, Paris.

© OECD 2001

A12. REPLACEMENT RATES

Definition and measurement

Setting the level of benefit payments raises many dilemmas for governments. On the one hand, too low a level can leave those in receipt of benefits in real distress. On the other, too high a level may leave individuals with little immediate financial incentive to seek work, potentially increasing benefit dependency and increasing the burden on taxpayers. One way of examining benefit payments to able-bodied people of working age across countries is to compare the benefit income of households after tax with what they would get were they to be earning a given percentage of the average wage. The ratio of the one to the other is known as the "net replacement rate". Table A12.1 compares incomes out of work with ⅔ of average earnings in each country, as this is close to the average re-entry wage across several countries (Arjona and Pearson, 2001).

Benefits often vary according to previous earnings and family type, and can also depend on factors such as family income and housing costs. In calculating the replacement rates presented here, it is assumed that short-term jobless people have sufficient assets to exclude them from receipt of means-tested benefits. Long-term jobless people, however, can receive means-tested benefits. Housing costs are assumed to be 20 per cent of average earnings in each country. OECD (1999) contains further detail on assumptions underlying the calculations.

Evidence and explanations

Replacement rates in the **first month** after losing employment are above 60% in all countries other than Greece, Italy, Korea and the United States. Indeed, they are above 80% in a significant number of countries, implying that the gain in income upon finding a job which pays just 2/3 of the average wage would yield relatively little increase in family income.

In the **longer term**, the pattern becomes more complicated. Insurance benefits run out (usually after between 6 months and 2 years of unemployment). But most countries have some form of "assistance" benefit – either unemployment assistance, or social assistance (the latter usually being administered by local governments). Assistance benefits are means-tested. However, in some Nordic countries they are often set at a level above two-thirds of average earnings, so the replacement rate is 100%. In other countries, there is a significant loss of income as families move from short-term to long-term benefits.

Childless households receive much lower benefit payments (Table A12.1), reflecting the general concern across OECD countries that children should not grow up in poverty.

The figures for several countries (Ireland, the UK, the USA) reflect the effects of policies which "**make work pay**". By giving families where someone works but where the family income is low a supplement through either the tax or benefit system, replacement rates are lowered without lowering out-of-work incomes.

Trends over time are difficult to calculate, but some idea can be gleaned from Chart A12.1. This does not take into account family benefits or the effects of taxation, but nevertheless gives the impression of a general upward trend in benefit entitlements, stabilising some time in the mid-1980s.

Status indicators: Employment (A1), Unemployment (A2), Relative poverty (B1), Low paid employment (B3).
Response indicators: Activation policies (A7), Minimum wages (B5), Public social spending (B6), Benefit recipiency (B9).

A12. REPLACEMENT RATES

Chart A12.1. OECD summary measure of benefit entitlements

As a percentage of expected earnings in work, 1961-1997

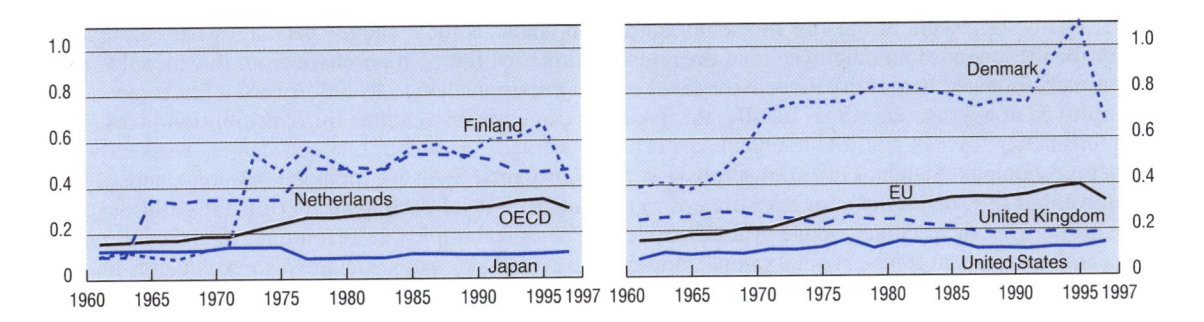

Table A12.1. Net replacement rates at the earnings level of 2/3 of an average production worker (after tax and including unemployment, family and housing benefits), 1999

	\multicolumn{4}{c}{In the first month of benefit receipt}	\multicolumn{4}{c}{For long-term benefit recipients}
	Single	Married couple	Couple 2 children	Lone parent 2 children	Single	Married couple	Couple 2 children	Lone parent 2 children
Australia	52	79	86	68	52	79	86	69
Austria	57	63	79	78	54	60	76	75
Belgium	84	76	75	81	61	88	79	85
Canada	62	65	69	67	35	57	77	77
Czech Republic	74	73	84	77	49	84	100	100
Denmark	89	94	95	89	67	94	92	82
Finland	72	84	94	93	79	100	100	84
France	83	82	86	86	55	56	60	60
Germany	69	71	74	78	75	85	61	82
Greece	55	50	48	52	0	0	5	6
Hungary	83	83	87	88	60	60	71	72
Iceland	77	70	87	89	74	100	100	82
Ireland	45	65	73	72	45	65	73	72
Italy	36	42	52	48	39	52	75	67
Japan	68	65	64	71	47	66	95	81
Korea	52	52	52	52	17	35	69	52
Luxembourg	82	81	87	87	67	91	91	83
Netherlands	92	89	90	86	84	93	94	84
Norway	65	67	74	84	52	88	73	82
Poland	56	57	61	59	53	51	55	57
Portugal	87	85	86	86	61	85	86	71
Spain	70	74	78	78	35	44	61	55
Sweden	77	77	90	96	84	100	100	100
Switzerland	73	72	84	84	88	93	93	85
United Kingdom	73	88	83	69	73	88	95	81
United States	59	59	51	51	10	18	61	51
OECD	**68.9**	**71.7**	**76.5**	**75.7**	**54.5**	**70.5**	**78.0**	**72.9**
EU	71.4	74.7	79.3	78.6	58.6	73.4	76.5	72.5

Source: OECD (1999).

Further reading

■ Arjona, R. and M. Pearson (2001, forthcoming), "Income changes when moving in and out of work", *Labour Market and Social Policy Occasional Papers*, Paris. ■ OECD (1999), *Benefit Systems and Work Incentives*, 1999 edition, Paris. ■ OECD (1997), *Making Work Pay*, Paris. ■ OECD (1994), *The Jobs Study: Evidence and Explanations*. ■ Pearson, M. and S. Scarpetta (2000), "What do we know about policies to make work pay?", *OECD Economic Studies*, No. 31, 2000/2, Paris.

A13. TAX WEDGE

Definition and measurement

The best measure of the size of the tax burden on labour is the "wedge" between what employers pay for the labour of an employee, and the consumption a worker can purchase from this income. The approach followed here is to calculate the taxes and contributions which would be paid when someone is employed at average earnings. Ideally, these calculations would account for consumption taxes, but unfortunately it is not possible to calculate a reliable average consumption tax burden for workers with average earnings. Standard tax allowances (*e.g.* for family members) are included but non-standard tax allowances (*e.g.* deductions for housing costs) are not. Universal cash benefits (*e.g.* for children) are deducted from the total tax wedge. Mandatory labour costs for employers that are not financed through general government funds, as for example employer-provided sick pay (B7), are also excluded from the calculations: for more detail see OECD (2000). Other measures of the tax burden on labour are useful: the labour tax ratio is defined as the sum of all labour tax revenue, expressed as a percentage of total wages and salaries and employers social security contributions.

Evidence and explanations

Considering the **tax burden on labour** is important as such taxes either raise the cost of employing labour, or reduce the financial returns to working. OECD (1994) evidences that the effects of taxing labour income depend to a great extent on wage-flexibility. If employer taxes go up, but wages do not fall, then the cost of labour rises and employment is likely to fall (A1). Higher unemployment (A2) may eventually depress wages. If, on the other hand, wages do fall, then unless benefits are also taxed (reducing living standards of those out of work), the effect will be to reduce the financial incentive to work (A12).

On average, the tax systems of OECD countries drive a wedge of 27% (for single earner married couples) or 37% (for single people) between what employers pay and what workers receive at average earnings (Table A13.1). **Cross-country variation** is substantial. Disposable income for single workers at average earnings is less than half of the amount which employers pay to employ such a person in Germany, Hungary, Sweden and Belgium, and the tax wedge is approaching that level in a number of other European countries. In most non-European OECD countries tax wedges are much lower.

The **extent of government interventions** to address social problems is ultimately constrained by the ability of government to raise funds. Changes in tax systems mean that overall tax revenue trends can differ from trends in taxation of different components (*e.g.* consumption and labour) or at different income levels. The tax-to-GDP ratio rose up until 1987, but has since stabilised (Chart A13.1). The average tax wedge and the labour tax ratio have both been rising, suggesting that there has been a shift towards greater reliance on labour taxes as a source of government revenue.

Status indicators: Employment (A1), Unemployment (A2), Income inequality (B2).
Response indicators: Replacement rates (A12), Public social expenditure (B6), Private social expenditure (B7).

A13. TAX WEDGE

Chart A13.1. **Tax wedge and tax ratios, 1978-1995 (average of sixteen countries)**

Index: 1978=100

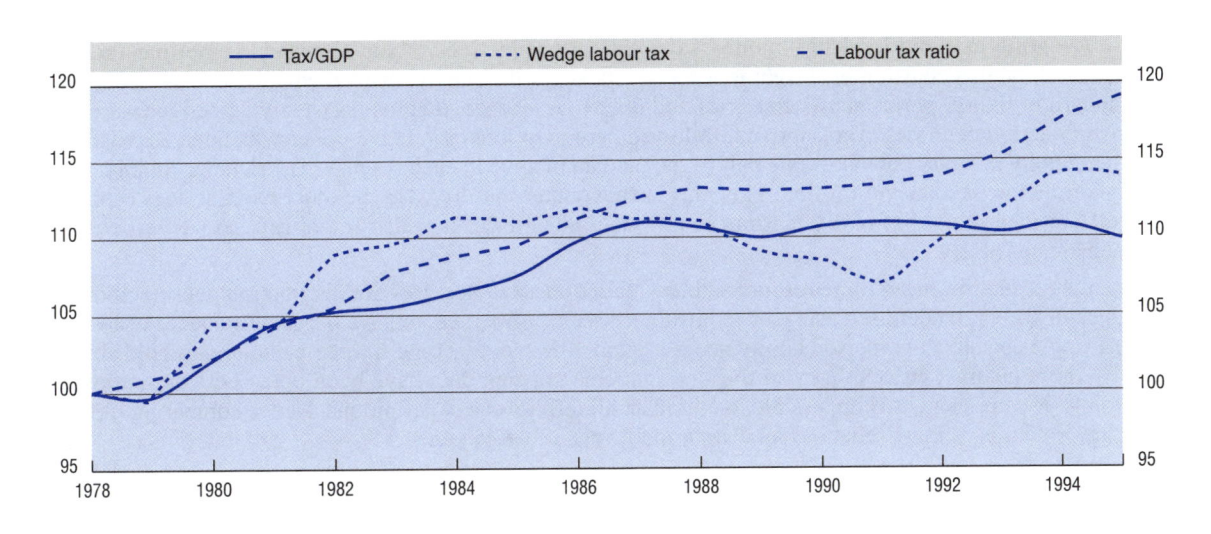

Sources: OECD (2000 and 2000a).

Table A13.1. **Total tax wedge including employer's social security contributions, 1999**

	Single	Married		Single	Married
Iceland	25.7	3.5	Spain	37.4	30.3
Luxembourg	35.0	11.4	Denmark	44.3	31.0
Korea	15.3	14.6	Turkey	31.1	31.1
Japan	19.3	14.7	Austria	46.0	31.8
New Zealand	19.4	15.0	Netherlands	44.4	34.2
Australia (1998)	25.4	15.5	Germany	51.9	34.5
Switzerland	29.8	17.6	Poland	41.0	34.8
Ireland	32.6	19.9	Hungary	50.6	35.3
Mexico	22.0	22.0	Greece	36.5	36.8
Canada	31.8	23.0	Italy	47.3	37.4
United Kingdom	31.0	23.8	France	47.9	38.8
United States	31.1	24.5	Finland	48.1	40.3
Czech Republic	42.8	25.5	Belgium	57.0	41.3
Portugal	33.4	26.0	Sweden	50.5	44.5
Norway	37.3	26.2			
OECD	**28.8**	**18.9**	EU	46.5	35.5

Source: OECD (2000a).

Further reading

■ OECD (2000), *Revenue Statistics, 1965-1999*, Paris. ■ OECD (2000a), *Taxing Wages, 1999 edition*, Paris. ■ OECD (1994), *OECD Jobs Study: Evidence and Explanations*, Paris.

B1. RELATIVE POVERTY

Definition and measurement

Avoiding material hardship is one of the primary objectives of social policy, sometimes made explicit through a constitutional right to a decent standard of living. However, what is seen as "a decent standard of living" varies across countries and over time. Hence, there is no widely agreed measure of poverty across countries. The approach followed here is to look at relative poverty, defined as existing when family incomes are below one half of the median income in each country. The richer a country, the higher the low-income cut-off line. This may seem counter-intuitive. On the other hand, it does capture well the idea that what really matters is not just subsistence but also the ability to participate in mainstream society.

Larger families need more resources than smaller ones. Hence, income distribution data (including indicator B2) is standardised using an "equivalence scale" of 0.5: *i.e.* to have the same standard of living as a single person, a two-person family needs around 40% more income, a three-person household about 70% more income, etc. On basis of the same income concept data have been obtained from national experts. Nevertheless, it is impossible to eliminate all differences in definitions. Hence comparing trends across countries is more reliable than comparing levels of low income.

Evidence and explanations

Perhaps surprisingly, there is **no common trend** in low-income rates over the ten years from the mid-1980s to the mid-1990s (Chart B1.1). Countries as Italy, the Netherlands and the United Kingdom experienced a clear rise in low-income rates, while low-income rates fell in other countries, including Australia, Canada and even the United States.

Low incomes are sensitive to the employment patterns and are thus related with age (A4, B3). The chance of having a low income varies dramatically according to **age** (Chart B1.2 – where the "relative poverty risk index" is the low-income share divided by population share for the relevant age group). Elderly people (not in work) are on average a third more likely to have low incomes than the population average, while prime age people (often workers), especially those aged between 51 and 65, are the least likely to have low incomes.

On the other hand, this risk of low income among the elderly has been falling sharply in recent years, while low-income rates among families with children edged up and rose sharply among young adults (Förster, 2000). These findings are related to **social expenditure** trends covering increased income support for the elderly, moderate growth in financial support to families with children, and a considerable reduction in benefit generosity for young adults (B6).

Most families could probably deal with a period of time on low incomes, as long as it did not last too long, while experiencing **poverty persistence** is far more difficult to cope with. Available evidence suggests (Table B1.1) that whereas a very high proportion of the population may be poor at least once in a six-year period, relatively few have a continuously low income. These few are at particular risk of exclusion.

Status indicators: Income inequality (B2), Low paid employment (B3), Jobless households (A4).
Response indicators: Public social expenditure (B6).

B1. RELATIVE POVERTY

Chart B1.1. **Proportion of people with low income, mid-1980s to mid-1990s**

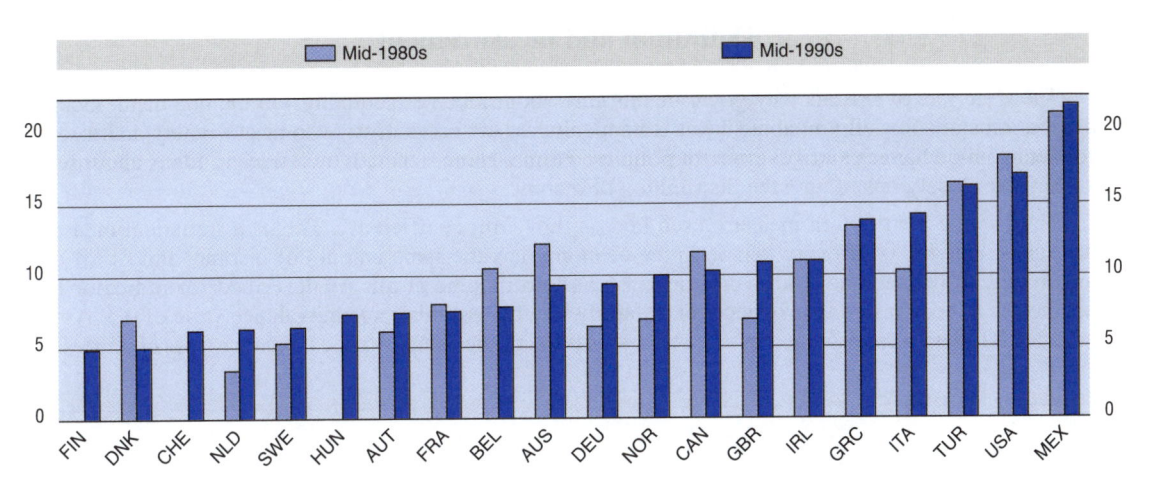

Chart B1.2. **Relative poverty risk indices by age group, mid-1980s to mid-1990s**

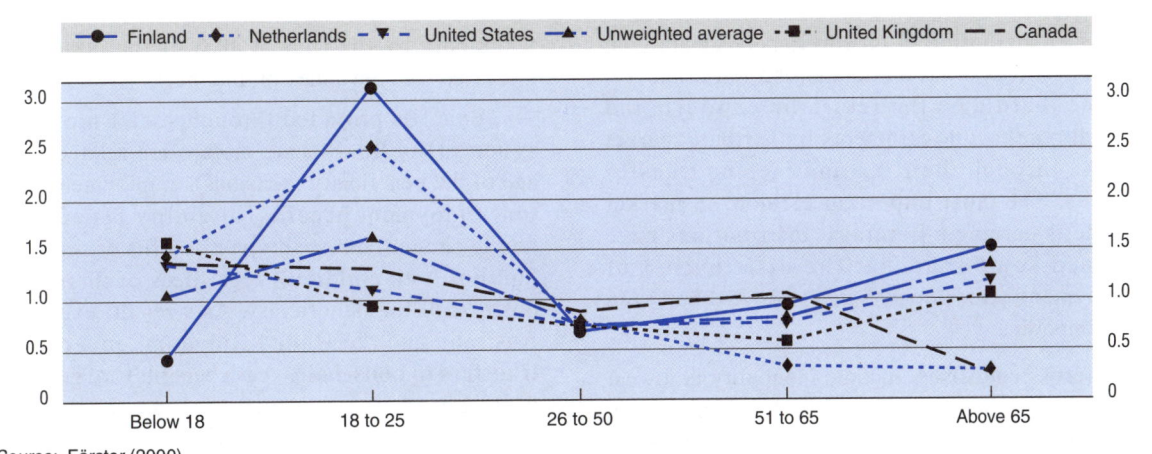

Source: Förster (2000).

Table B1.1. **Poverty persistence: percentage of the population which is poor over or during a six-year period**

	Studied period	Average poverty rates	Continuously poor	Poor at least once
Canada	1990-95	11.4	1.8	28.1
Germany	1991-96	10.2	1.8	19.9
Netherlands	1991-96	6.1	0.8	12.1
Sweden	1991-96	7.4	1.1	11.9
United Kingdom	1991-96	20	6.1	38.4
United States	1988-93	14.2	4.6	26

Source: Oxley et al. (2000).

Further reading

■ Arjona, R., M. Ladaique and M. Pearson (2001), "Growth, inequality and social protection", Labour Market and Social Policy Occasional Paper, No. 51, OECD, Paris. ■ Atkinson, A., L. Rainwater and T. Smeeding (1995), *Income Distribution in OECD Countries,* OECD Social Policy Studies No. 18, Paris. ■ Förster, M. (2000), "Trends and driving factors in income distribution and poverty in the OECD area", Labour Market and Social Policy Occasional Paper, No. 42, OECD, Paris. ■ OECD (2001), *Employment Outlook,* Paris. ■ Oxley, H., T. Thanh Dang and P. Antolin (2000), "Poverty dynamics in six OECD countries", *OECD Economic Studies,* No. 30, 2000/1.

B2. INCOME INEQUALITY

Definition and measurement

There are lots of reasons why governments care about income inequality. On the one hand, income distribution statistics tell you about what is happening in the economy – who are "winners and losers" from economic changes and government policies. From a more normative viewpoint, ideas about what is "fair" are closely linked with the distribution of income.

The income distribution measure used here is the "Gini coefficient". This is a statistical measure that has a value of "0" if every person in the economy has the same amount of income, and "1" if one person had all the income, and everybody else had no income at all. As described for indicator B1, income has to be adjusted to take account of family size by assuming an equivalence scale of 0.5. As for indicator B1, data were provided by national experts using the same income concept across countries.

Evidence and explanations

The **distribution of income** depends mainly on two things: first of all on the distribution of *market* income (earnings, the return on capital), and secondly on how governments redistribute market income through their tax and income transfer policies. The most important element in market income is earnings. Earnings' distributions have widened somewhat, but the distribution of employment across households (A1, A4) has been more important.

Across countries, income inequality is lowest in the Nordic countries (Chart B2.1). It is highest in those OECD countries with the lowest per capita incomes – Mexico and Turkey, with Greece not far behind. On balance, the distribution of income has widened a bit in the ten years between the mid-1980s and the mid-1990s. But the **trend** is not a strong one, and indeed there are several countries where the income distribution has narrowed (Australia, Canada, Finland and Ireland).

The **distribution of market income** is very uneven, with less than 10% of all such income being received by the bottom 30% income earners, while taxes mirror the distribution of market income (Table B2.1). Over the mid-80s to the mid-90s, the trend has been towards more market income inequality in every country, while the proportion of taxes paid by the richest 30% of the population increased (see the annex on Internet).

Benefits provided through social protection systems (B6, B8, B9) are more often related to the age of the beneficiary (pensions), employment status (unemployment benefits, disability benefits), or family circumstances (survivor benefits or support to families with children), regardless of the income position of the beneficiary. As a result, except for Australia and the United Kingdom, **government transfers to households** (cash benefits) are generally distributed quite evenly across the income distribution (Table B2.1). Families across the income distribution often receive similar amounts of benefit income, but because those at the bottom of the distribution have little market income, net (after tax) benefit income is much more important in determining their standard of living. Taxes reduce household income. Most direct income taxes are paid by those in the upper income deciles.

Status indicators: Employment (A1), Jobless households (A4), Relative poverty (B1), Low paid employment (B3).
Response indicators: Replacement rates (A12), Public social expenditure (B6), Net social expenditure (B8), Benefit recipiency (B9).

B2. INCOME INEQUALITY

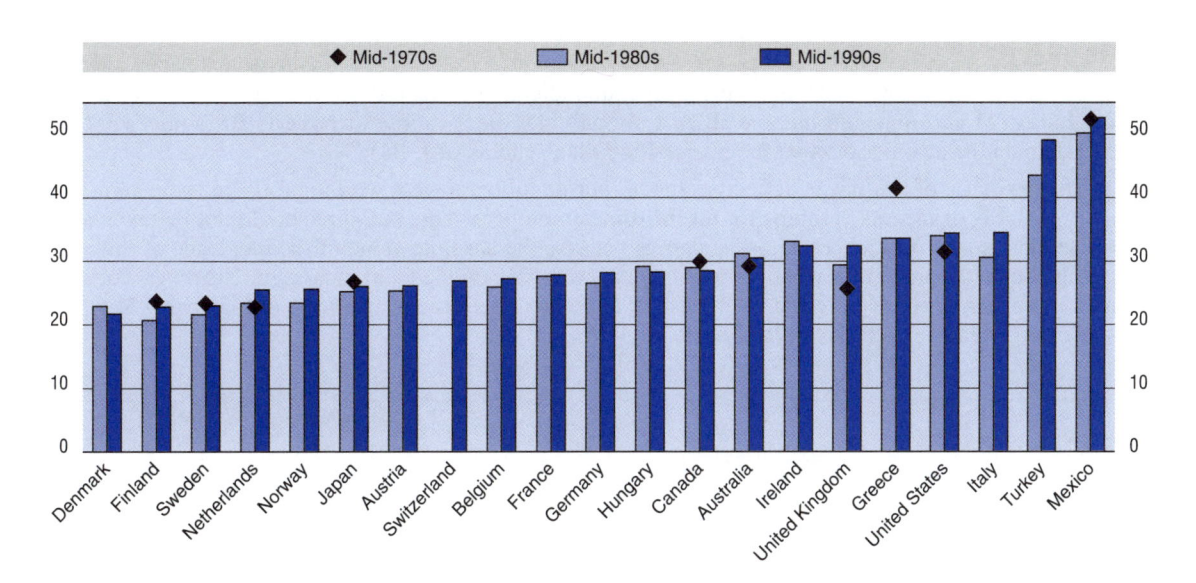

Chart B2.1. **Evolution of the Gini coefficient between mid-1970s and mid-1990s**

Table B2.1. **Sources of income of the working age population, mid-1990s**

	Market income			General government transfers			Taxes		
	Three bottom deciles	Four middle deciles	Three top deciles	Three bottom deciles	Four middle deciles	Three top deciles	Three bottom deciles	Four middle deciles	Three top deciles
Australia	7.4	36.0	56.6	62.3	31.1	6.5	3.7	31.1	65.1
Belgium	7	34	59	36	42	23	4	33	64
Canada	9.6	35.5	54.9	41.5	37.7	20.8	6.2	33.4	60.4
Denmark	11.4	37.8	50.8	43.4	38.9	17.7	14.1	37.2	48.7
Finland	10.2	35.6	54.2	43.2	40.4	16.4	9.8	33.4	56.8
France	10.9	33.5	55.6	35.6	39.3	25.1	8.7	23.5	67.9
Germany	11.9	36.3	51.8	31.7	37.6	30.7	10.0	36.5	53.6
Greece	12	34	54	21	38	42			
Hungary	9	32	59	29	43	29			
Ireland	5.7	33.2	61.1	47.1	38.1	14.8	3.3	30.3	66.4
Italy	9.0	31.9	59.1	20.5	45.0	34.5	6.7	31.0	62.3
Mexico	6	24	69	14	27	59			
Netherlands	10.0	37.1	52.8	45.8	36.1	18.1	11.7	36.1	52.2
Norway	11.7	37.3	51.0	45.6	35.9	18.6	10.2	36.1	53.7
Sweden	9.3	36.9	53.9	33.7	40.5	25.8	11.0	35.8	53.3
Turkey	8	24	68	15	40	45			
United Kingdom	7.7	35.0	57.3	55.0	32.8	12.2	5.6	34.2	60.2
United States	8.9	33.9	57.1	41.4	35.5	23.0	6.3	28.4	65.3

Source: Förster (2000).

Further reading

■ Atkinson, A., L. Rainwater and T. Smeeding (1995), *Income Distribution in OECD Countries,* OECD Social Policy Studies No. 18. ■ Förster, M. (2000) "Trends and driving factors in income distribution and poverty in the OECD area", OECD Labour Market and Social Policy Occasional Paper No. 42, OECD, Paris. ■ OECD (2000), *Social Expenditure Database*, Paris.

B3. LOW PAID EMPLOYMENT

Definition and measurement

The incidence of low-paid employment gives an indication of the differences across countries in the distribution of earnings and income (B2). Low pay may be a source of poverty for some workers depending on the incomes of other members of their households (A4, B1).

The incidence of low pay is defined as the proportion of employees working full-time who earn less than two-thirds of median earnings for all full-time employees. This measure should not be taken as a precise indicator of differences across countries because the absolute value of the incidence of low pay in each country can be quite sensitive to the way low pay is defined and measured. However, country rankings appear to be less affected by the use of alternative definitions and ways of measuring low pay (Keese and Puymoyen, 2001, forthcoming).

Evidence and explanations

The incidence of low pay ranges from a low of 5 to 7 per cent in Sweden, Finland and Belgium to a high of 20 to 25 per cent in the United Kingdom, Canada, Ireland and the United States (Chart B3.1). There is considerable similarity **across countries** in the characteristics of workers and types of sectors that are associated with a high risk of low pay, such as youths, women, unskilled workers and workers in retail and wholesale trade and in hotels and restaurants (OECD, 1996).

Trends reveal that since the mid-1970s the incidence of low pay has risen in several, but not all, OECD countries (Chart B3.2). Particularly large increases occurred during the 1990s in the Central and Eastern European countries, such as Hungary and Poland, reflecting a large rise in earnings inequality in these countries.

Country differences in the incidence of low pay are closely **linked** to the overall degree of **earnings inequality**: countries with greater earnings inequality tend to have a higher incidence of low-paid jobs (Chart B3.1). The underlying distribution of earnings in each country is related to the distribution of skills (A10, A11) which is in turn related to the performance of education and training systems, the composition of final demand and trends in migration, trade and technological change. Institutional settings also play a role: a low incidence of low pay tends to be associated with relatively high statutory minimum wages (B5) and/or generous welfare benefits (A12), and with widespread union and/or collective bargaining coverage (Bardone, Gittleman and Keese, 1998; Kahn, 2000).

Not all low-paid workers are stuck in low-paying jobs. In all countries there is substantial **mobility** out of low pay, especially for younger workers (OECD, 1996, 1997). However, certain core groups such as unskilled workers and older workers face a relatively high risk of remaining stuck in a low-paid job. Moreover, not all moves out of low pay are into higher-paying jobs but, in many instances, consist of a move out of employment altogether. The degree of earnings mobility appears to be rather uniform across countries: countries with a higher incidence of low pay do not necessarily display a higher degree of mobility out of low pay.

Status indicators: Employment (A1), Jobless households (A4), Relative poverty (B1), Income inequality (B2), Gender wage gap (B4).
Response indicators: Educational attainment (A10), Literacy (A11), Replacement rates (A12), Minimum wages (B5).

B3. LOW PAID EMPLOYMENT

Chart B3.1. Incidence of low pay and earnings dispersion, mid- to late 1990s

Incidence: Percentage of full-time workers earning less than two-thirds of full-time median earnings
Earnings dispersion: Ratio of 9th decile earnings to 1st decile earnings for all full-time workers

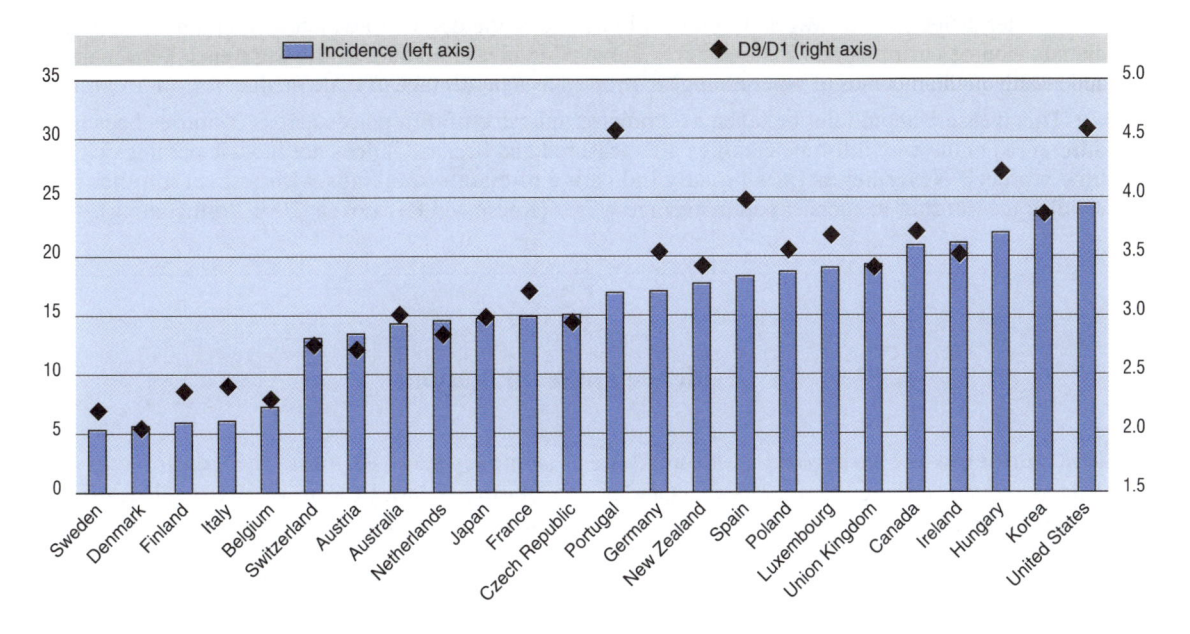

Chart B3.2. Trends in the incidence of low pay in selected OECD countries, 1975-1999

Percentage of full-time workers earning less than two-thirds of full-time median earnings

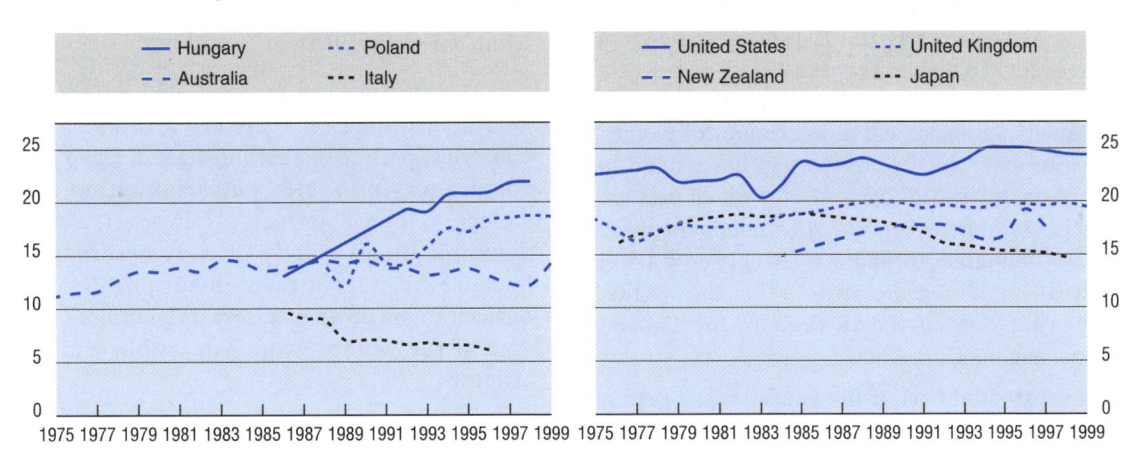

Source: OECD Structure of Earnings Database, see Keese and Puymoyen (2001, forthcoming).

Further reading

- Bardone, L, M. Gittleman and M. Keese (1998), "Causes and consequences of earnings inequality in OECD countries", *Lavoro e Relazioni Industriali*, No. 2, July-December. ■ Kahn, L.M. (2000), "Wage inequality, collective bargaining, and relative employment from 1985 to 1994: Evidence from fifteen OECD countries", *The Review of Economics and Statistics*, 82(4), November, pp. 564-579. ■ Keese, M. and A. Puymoyen (2001, forthcoming), "Changes in earnings structure: Some international comparisons using the OECD structure of earnings database", OECD Labour Market and Social Policy Occasional Papers. ■ OECD (1997), "Earnings mobility: Taking a longer run view", in *OECD Employment Outlook*, Paris, July. ■ OECD (1996), "Earnings inequality, low-paid employment and earnings mobility", in *OECD Employment Outlook*, Paris, July.

B4. GENDER WAGE GAP

Definition and measurement

Gender differences in wages provide an indicator of the degree to which men and women receive similar incomes from work. The "gender wage gap" is measured here as the difference between male and female median full-time time earnings expressed as a percentage of male median full-time earnings.

This measure should not be taken as a precise indicator of differences across countries because of differences in the way full-time earnings are measured and because it does not include earnings of part-time workers. Nevertheless, it is broadly indicative of country rankings with respect to other more detailed measures of the gender gap in average wages (Keese and Puymoyen, 2001, forthcoming).

Evidence and explanations

The **gender wage gap** within and across countries is related to three main factors: *i)* gender differences in employment with respect to sector, occupation, firm size, skills, job tenure and overall work experience (A1, A10, A11); *ii)* the returns to each of these factors in terms of relative wages; and *iii)* discrimination. In turn, market forces and national social and institutional settings affect each of these three factors.

Across countries, the gender wage gap ranges from a low of between 11 and 12 per cent in Belgium and Denmark to a high of between 39 and 41 per cent in Japan and Korea (Chart B4.1). Reflecting a rise in educational attainment and in job tenure for women relative to men, the size of the gap has tended to decline **over time** in all countries for which data are available, with the exception of Sweden where the gap has fluctuated around a relatively low level (Chart B4.2). Since the mid-1970s, the largest declines have occurred in France, the United Kingdom and the United States.

A substantial part of the gender wage gap in each country, and part of the differences between countries, can be accounted for by gender differences in the **composition of the workforce**. For example, these differences appear to be particularly large in Japan and are probably more important in accounting for its relatively large gender wage gap than any systematic underpaying of women *vis-à-vis* men in similar types of employment. In fact, the gender gap in mean starting salaries for university graduates in Japan is relatively small (around 4 per cent in 1999).

The **overall** degree of **wage inequality** in each country also underpins, and possibly accounts for much of, the cross-country variation in the size of the gender wage gap (Blau and Kahn, 2000). To the extent that women are disproportionately represented among low-paid workers (B3, B5), the gender wage gap tends to be larger where earnings inequality is wider (Gregory, 1999).

Despite equal pay for equal work provisions and anti-discrimination legislation in most OECD countries, part of the earnings gender gap in each country may also reflect **discrimination** against women in the labour market. However, given that discrimination is rarely directly observable and because of other measurement problems, it is difficult to pin down precisely its contribution to the size of the gender wage gap within and across countries.

Status indicators: Employment (A1), Relative poverty (B1), Income inequality (B2), Low paid employment (B3).
Response indicators: Minimum wages (B5), Educational attainment (A10), Literacy (A11).

B4. GENDER WAGE GAP

Chart B4.1. Gender wage gap, mid- to late 1990s

Difference between male and female median full-time earnings as a per cent of male median full-time earnings

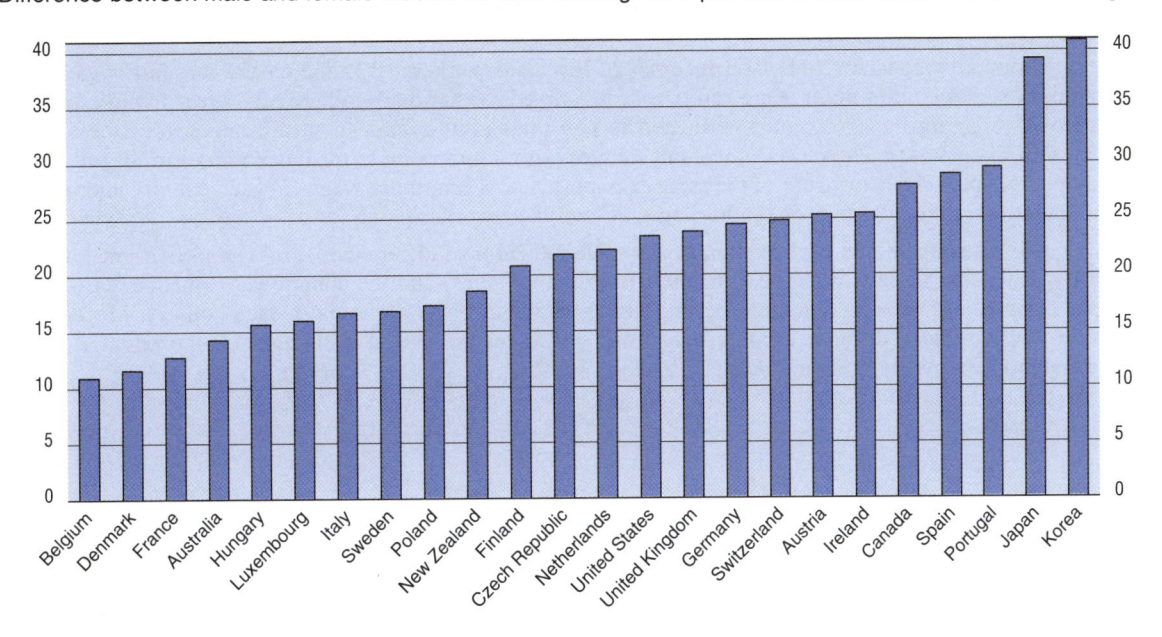

Chart B4.2. Trends in gender wage gap in selected OECD countries, 1975-1999

Difference between male and female median full-time earnings as a per cent of male median full-time earnings

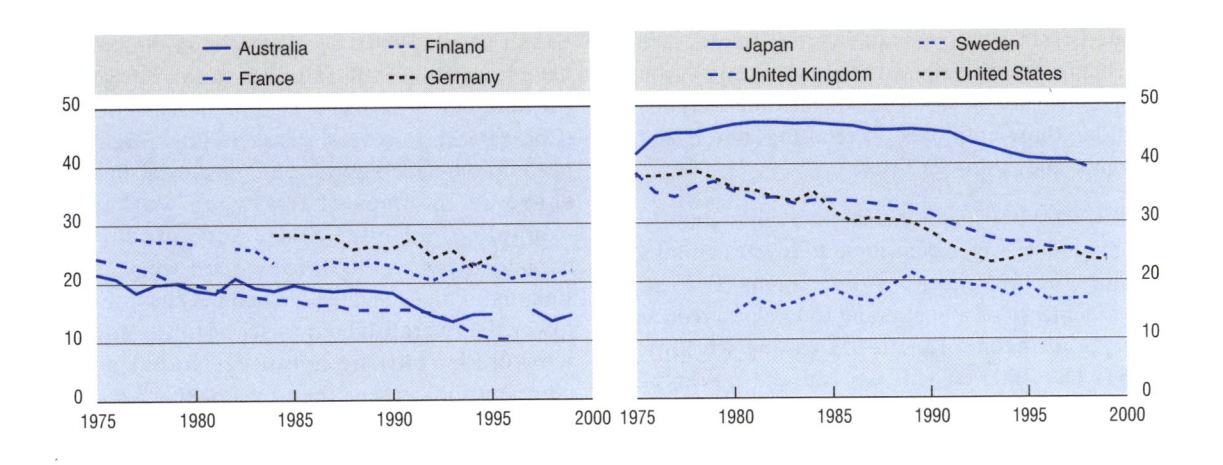

Source: OECD Structure of Earnings Database, see Keese and Puymoyen (2001, forthcoming).

Further reading

■ Blau, F.D. and L.M. Kahn (2000), "Gender differences in pay", NBER Working Paper Series, Working Paper 7732, June. ■ Gregory, B. (1999), "Labour market institutions and the gender pay ratio", *The Australian Economic Review*, Vol. 32, No. 3, pp. 273-278. ■ Keese, M. and A. Puymoyen (2001, forthcoming), "Changes in earnings structure: Some international comparisons using the OECD structure of earnings database", OECD Labour Market and Social Policy Occasional Papers, OECD, Paris.

© OECD 2001

B5. MINIMUM WAGES

Definition and measurement

Minimum wages aim to bolster incomes of low-paid workers (B3) and ensure that fair wages are paid. A statutory minimum wage refers to a legislated, or national collectively-agreed, wage levels below which employers are not permitted to pay their employees: such minima currently exist in 21 OECD countries. The ratio of the adult statutory minimum wage to median earnings of all full-time employees provides a measure of the relative importance of minimum wages in each country and of the extent to which it helps to prop up the wages of low-wage workers.

This measure should not be taken as a precise indicator of differences across countries since it can vary depending on how both the numerator (minimum wages) and the denominator (median earnings) are defined and measured and on the underlying distribution of earnings in each country. Moreover, there are substantial differences in the way minimum wages are set and operate, and in the extent of their differentiation by age or region (OECD, 1998).

Evidence and explanations

Relative to median wages for full-time employees, adult minimum wages appear to be highest in France and Australia, and lowest in Korea and Mexico (Chart B5.1). Relatively few countries are able to provide information on the incidence and distribution of employment at minimum wages. But a number of similarities can be identified: the incidence of minimum-wage work tends to be highest among youth, women and part-time workers, and among those employed in retailing, hotels and restaurants, and in smaller firms.

OECD (1998) suggests that, on a cross-country basis, minimum wages contribute to lower earnings inequality, smaller gender pay differentials (B4) and a lower incidence of low pay, and can help to reduce **poverty and income inequality** among working families (B1, B2, B3). However, the poverty-alleviating impact of minimum wages more generally is limited as many poor families are jobless households (A4) while many minimum-wage workers live in households with above-average incomes.

By setting a floor to wages above market-clearing levels, a statutory minimum wage can also lead to lower employment than would otherwise be the case (A1, A3), but there is no general agreement on the extent to which this occurs in practice.

Negative employment effects are most likely to occur when minimum wages are set at a relatively high level compared to average earnings, especially for low-wage workers such as youth and unskilled workers. Countries have sought to mitigate these possible "**disemployment**" effects in a number of ways (Keese, 1998). For example, minimum wages have been allowed to fall relative to average wages (or total labour costs) over time in many countries (Chart B5.2). In several instances, these trends have been accompanied by offsetting mechanisms to help shore up incomes of low-wage workers. For example, the United States has introduced and expanded tax credits for low-paid workers while Belgium, France and the Netherlands have sought to lower the overall labour costs of hiring low-wage workers by cutting employer social security contributions rather than by lowering minimum wages in absolute or relative terms (A12, A13).

Status indicators: Employment (A1), Jobless youth (A3), Jobless households (A4), Relative poverty (B1), Income inequality (B2), Low paid employment (B3), Gender wage gap (B4).
Response indicators: Replacement rates (A12), Tax wedge (A13).

B5. MINIMUM WAGES

Chart B5.1. Ratio of adult minimum wages to median full-time earnings, mid-2000

Chart B5.2. Trends in the ratio of adult minimum wages to median full-time earnings, 1975-2000

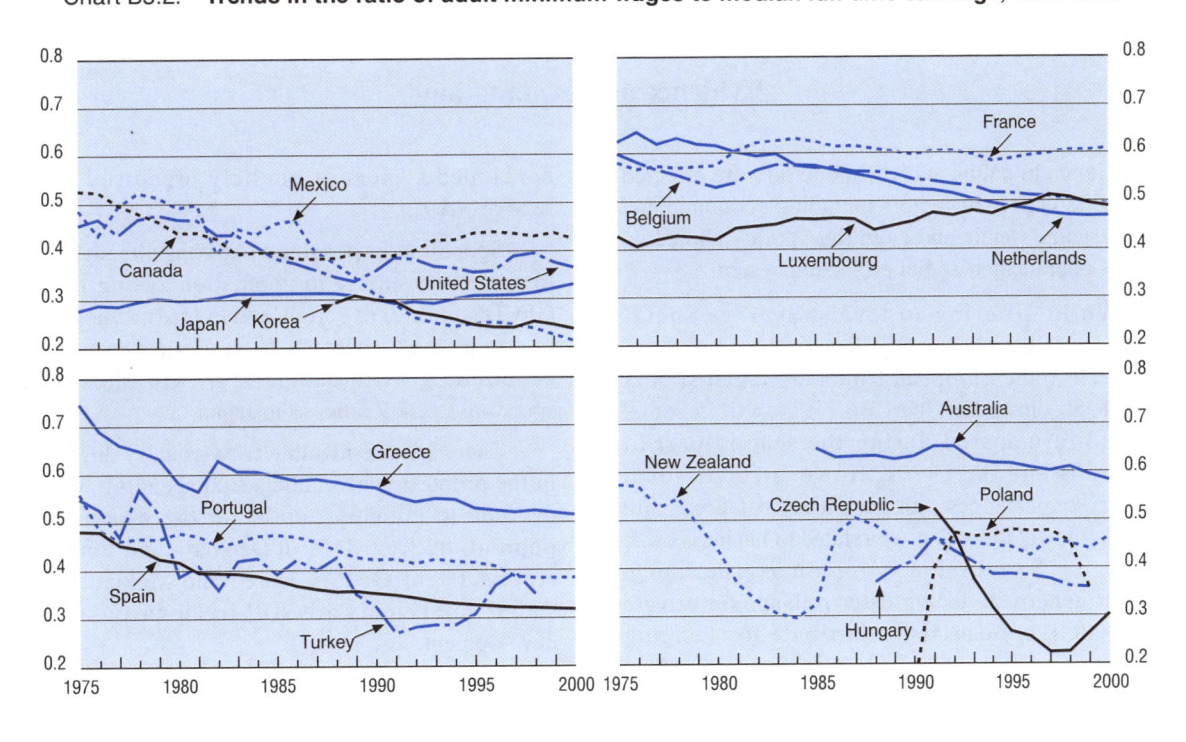

Source: OECD Structure of Earnings Database, see Keese and Puymoyen (2001, forthcoming).

Further reading

- Keese, M. (1998), "Are statutory minimum wages an endangered species?", in C. Lucifora and W. Salverda (eds.), *Policies for Low Wage Employment and Social Exclusion*, Franco Angeli, Milan. ■ Keese, M. and A. Puymoyen (2001, forthcoming), "Changes in earnings structure: Some international comparisons using the OECD structure of earnings database", OECD Labour Market and Social Policy Occasional Papers, OECD, Paris. ■ OECD (1998), "Making the most of the minimum: Statutory minimum wages, employment and poverty", in *OECD Employment Outlook*, Paris, June.

© OECD 2001

B6. PUBLIC SOCIAL EXPENDITURE

Definition and measurement

For cross-country comparisons, the most commonly used indicator of what governments re-allocate to social effort is public social expenditure related to GDP. Public social expenditure is defined as the provision by public institutions of benefits to, and financial contributions targeted at, households and individuals in order to provide support during circumstances which adversely affect their welfare, provided that the provision of the benefits and financial contributions constitutes neither a direct payment for a particular good or service nor an individual contract or transfer. Such benefits can be cash transfers, or can be the direct ("in-kind") provision of goods and services.

Public social expenditure has been grouped along the following broad spending categories: pensions (old-age cash benefits and survivors); income support to the working age population (disability cash benefits, occupational injury and disease, sickness benefits, family cash benefits, unemployment benefits, housing benefits and other contingencies); public health expenditure (C7) and other social services (services for the elderly and disabled people, family services and active labour market policies). The data concern gross (before tax) expenditure items (B7, B8). Measurement problems do exist, particularly with regard to spending by lower tiers of government.

Evidence and explanations

Trends in public social expenditure are affected by a wide variety of factors including economic and demographic trends and countries' policy choice on how to operate their social protection system.

While differing in levels, average social expenditure **trends** for OECD countries and those affiliated to the European Union are rather similar from 1980 onwards (Chart B6.1): growth in social expenditure abated during the second part of the 1980s and the 1990s. However, individual country experiences can be widely different and remarkable volatility is often related to business cycle trends, *e.g.* Sweden. Policy reform, *e.g.* declining benefit generosity or a greater reliance on private sector delivery can also contribute to changing spending patterns, as for example in New Zealand.

Public social expenditure **levels** are considerably larger in Europe than in most non-European OECD countries (Chart B6.2). On average, public spending on social services (including health care) is about 50% of spending on public cash transfers, with Nordic countries spending considerably more, in part because of their well-developed system of publicly organised family services (A9).

Spending on **pensions** (A6) has already started to grow in response to population ageing in some OECD countries (*e.g.* Italy and France), although this is sometimes difficult to discern as sustained economic growth dampens growth rates of the spending to GDP ratio, as in Japan.

There are considerable cross-country differences in the proportion of public social spending which is devoted to income support for the **working age population**: from 10% in Denmark and Finland to around 1% of GDP in Korea and Mexico, where social safety-nets are still in an early stage of development.

Status indicators: Unemployment (A2), Retirement ages (A6), Relative poverty (B1).
Response indicators: Activation policies (A7), Early childhood education and care (A9), Private Social expenditure (B7), Net social expenditure (B8), Benefit recipiency (B9), Health care expenditure (C7).

B6. PUBLIC SOCIAL EXPENDITURE

Chart B6.1. Public social spending for selected countries, 1980-1997
Per cent of GDP

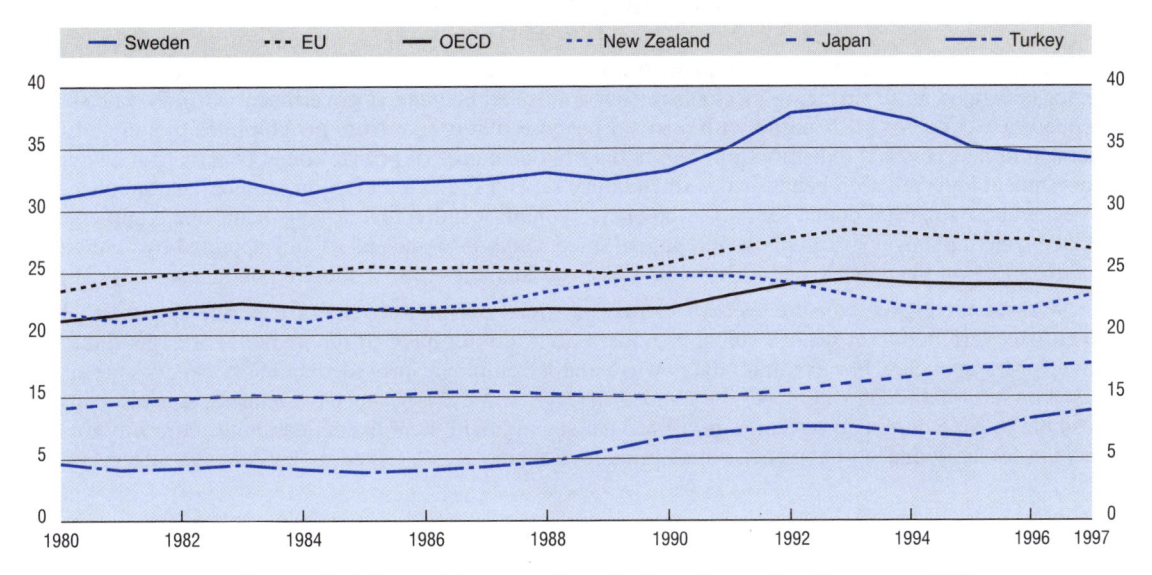

Legend: Sweden — EU --- OECD — New Zealand --- Japan -- Turkey -·-

Chart B6.2. Public social expenditure by broad social policy area, 1997
Per cent of GDP

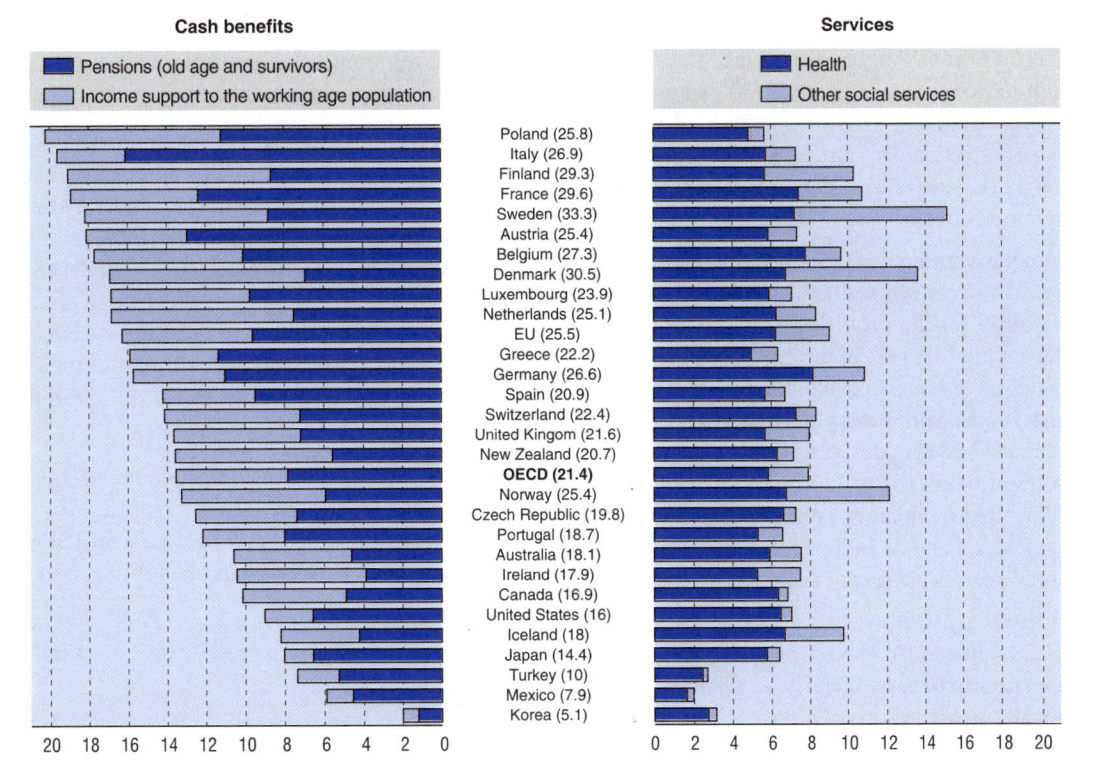

Cash benefits
- Pensions (old age and survivors)
- Income support to the working age population

Services
- Health
- Other social services

Countries (total % of GDP):
- Poland (25.8)
- Italy (26.9)
- Finland (29.3)
- France (29.6)
- Sweden (33.3)
- Austria (25.4)
- Belgium (27.3)
- Denmark (30.5)
- Luxembourg (23.9)
- Netherlands (25.1)
- EU (25.5)
- Greece (22.2)
- Germany (26.6)
- Spain (20.9)
- Switzerland (22.4)
- United Kingom (21.6)
- New Zealand (20.7)
- **OECD (21.4)**
- Norway (25.4)
- Czech Republic (19.8)
- Portugal (18.7)
- Australia (18.1)
- Ireland (17.9)
- Canada (16.9)
- United States (16)
- Iceland (18)
- Japan (14.4)
- Turkey (10)
- Mexico (7.9)
- Korea (5.1)

Source: OECD (2000), *Social Expenditure Database, 1980-1997*, Paris.

Further reading

■ OECD (2001, forthcoming), *Social and Health Policy Analysis*, Paris. ■ OECD (2000), *OECD Social Expenditure Database, 1980-1997*, Paris. ■ OECD (1999), *A Caring World, The New Social Policy Agenda*, Paris. ■ OECD (1997), *Family, Market and Community: Equity and Efficiency in Social Policy*, Paris.

© OECD 2001

B7. PRIVATE SOCIAL EXPENDITURE

Definition and measurement

Households can receive social support from both the public and private sectors, where the private sector is defined as all financing mechanisms not controlled by general government (B6). Private social expenditure concerns all benefits with a social purpose that derive from programmes that contain an element of interpersonal redistribution. The re-distributive nature of private social benefits can be due to government legislation on benefit rules (mandatory private social benefits) or stipulations in collective agreements or financial public support to otherwise voluntary individual arrangements and employment-related benefit plans. For example, employment-based health insurance plans are supported by favourable tax treatment worth around 1% of GDP in the US, a considerable redistribution of public resources (B8).

Measurement problems are greater for private social expenditure than for public spending (B6). Even if governments set benefit rules, providers often do not have to report relevant expenditure to government agencies. For example, data on mandatory employer-provided sickness benefits are often based on information on wages and the number of days' work lost because of sickness. It is also not yet possible to have complete coverage of all private social health benefits, as estimates currently do not account for individual co-payments, where price-levels have been affected by government intervention.

Evidence and explanations

There are considerable differences in the extent to which national social protection system rely on private provision, and in some countries at least, the role of private benefits appears to be growing in importance (Chart B7.1). There are different factors underlying this trend.

Some governments (Denmark, the Netherlands and Sweden) legislated increased employer's responsibility for the provision of sickness benefits (B9) during the first part of the 1990s, while German employers have been responsible for such benefits since the 1960s. **Mandatory private social benefits** also concern benefits deriving from regulations on occupational accidents and diseases (*e.g.* in Australia), and mandatory pension contributions to employer-based and/or individual pension plans, as, for example, in Switzerland (Table B7.1).

Maturing private pension programmes are largely responsible for the upward trend in **private social expenditure**, especially in Canada, where pension plans are relatively mature compared to other countries. The size of employment-related social benefits (sickness and incapacity related income support) that top-up public and mandatory private benefits is related to changes in the generosity of publicly controlled benefits, and have gained in importance since the 1980s.

Private health-care is much more important in the United States than in any other OECD country. The private social expenditure trend for the United States thus reflects significantly increasing health-care costs during the 1980s. A decline in the proportion of employers in the United States who provide health care coverage (and a reduction of benefit rates) also contributed to the limited growth of private social expenditure in the United States during the first part of the 1990s.

As capitalised pension programmes are gaining in importance in many OECD countries and as these programmes have yet to fully **mature**, the importance of private social benefits is expected to grow.

Status indicators: Employment (A1), Income inequality (B2).
Response indicators: Public social expenditure (B6), Net social expenditure (B8), Health care expenditure (C7), Responsibility for financing health care (C8).

B7. PRIVATE SOCIAL EXPENDITURE

Chart B7.1. **Private social expenditure, 1980-1995**

Per cent of GDP

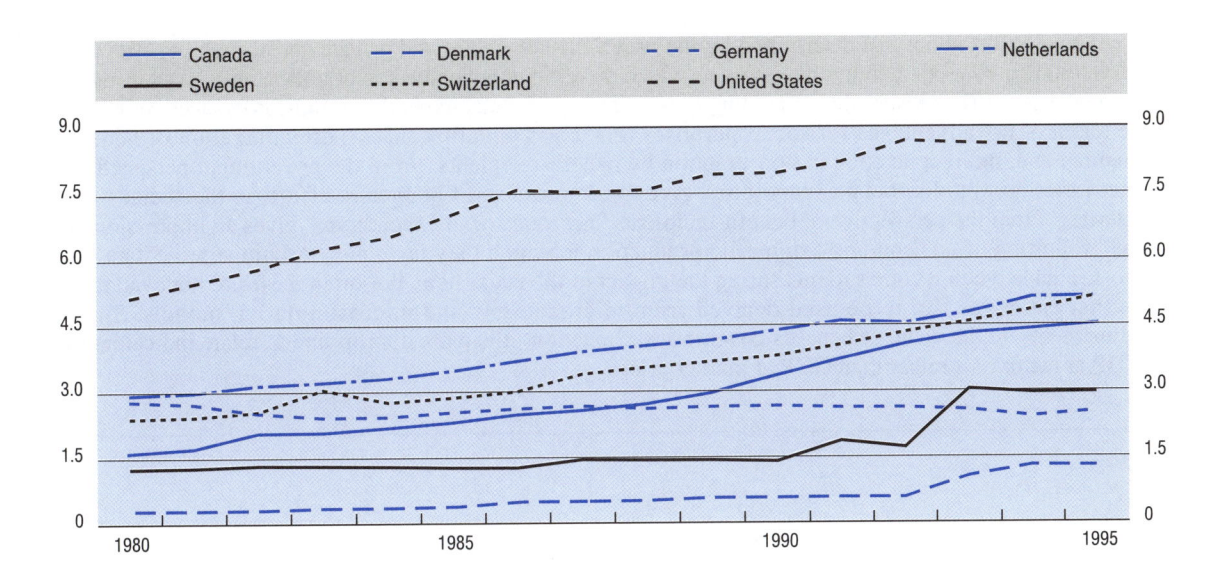

Table B7.1. **Private social expenditure in selected OECD countries, 1995**

	Mandatory private social	Voluntary private social – Cash benefits	Voluntary private social – Health	Total private social	Total private social as a share in all social expenditure
Australia	1.1	1.9	0.9	3.9	18
Belgium	1.5	0.4	0.5	2.4	8
Canada		3.6	0.9	4.5	20
Denmark	0.4	0.7	0.1	1.3	4
Finland	0.2	1.1	0.1	1.4	4
Germany	1.6	0.8	0.1	2.5	8
Ireland		1.2	0.6	1.8	8
Italy		1.6	0.2	1.8	7
Netherlands	0.8	3.1	1.2	5.1	16
Sweden	0.4	2.5	0.1	3.0	8
Switzerland	4.3	0.0	0.8	5.1	20
United Kingdom	0.2	3.5	0.3	4.0	15
United States	0.5	3.0	5.0	8.6	34

Source: Adema (1999).

Further reading

■ Adema, W. (2000), "Revisiting real social spending across countries: A brief note", *OECD Economic Studies*, No. 30, 2000/01, Paris. ■ OECD (2000), *OECD Social Expenditure Database, 1980-1997*, Paris. ■ Adema, W. (1999), "Net total social expenditure", Labour Market and Social Policy Occasional Paper, No. 39, Paris. ■ Adema, W. and M. Einerhand (1998), "The growing role of private social benefits", Labour Market and Social Policy Occasional Paper, No. 32, OECD, Paris.

B8. NET SOCIAL EXPENDITURE

Definition and measurement

Social effort is not just determined by the prevalence of public and private social cash benefits and services (B6, B7), but also by the extent to which governments pursue social policy objectives through the tax system. To measure this effect on gross (before tax) social expenditure indicators, account has to be taken of tax advantages for social purposes (*e.g.* child tax allowances); direct taxation of benefit income; and, indirect taxation of consumption by benefit-recipients. From the government perspective, "net (after tax) public social expenditure" gives an impression of budgetary efforts in the social field after tax. From the perspective of benefit-recipients "net total social expenditure" gives an impression of the proportion of an economy's domestic production to which they lay claim. Administrative data are most reliable when it comes to measuring the impact of the tax system, but often these are not available, so that estimates had to be used derived from microdatasets and microsimulation models. Since adjustments on the value of benefits cover indirect taxation, it is more appropriate to relate indicators to GDP at factor cost rather than GDP at market prices.

Evidence and explanations

Direct taxes and social security contributions establish a much larger burden on benefit income in the Netherlands and the Nordic countries than elsewhere (Table B8.1). Private pension benefits (B7) are taxed heavily in Canada, Denmark, Finland, the Netherlands, and Sweden while the average tax burden on these benefits is relatively light in the other countries.

The value of benefit income clawed back through **indirect taxation** is much larger in European countries than in Australia, Canada and the United States.

Countries with relatively limited direct taxation levies on benefit income – Australia, Canada, Germany, Ireland, the UK and the US, make more extensive use of **tax breaks for social purposes** (TBSP) (not including those for pensions) than countries with high direct tax burdens on benefit income.

In general, governments claw back more money through direct and indirect taxation of public transfer income than the value of the tax advantages awarded for social purposes, except for the United States where gross public spending actually **underestimates** public social effort.

Gross public social expenditure indicators lead us to believe that public social effort is about 10 percentage points higher in continental western European and Nordic countries than in non-European OECD countries (Chart B8.1). Accounting for tax systems and private social benefits leads to **convergence** of social expenditure levels across countries: recipients of social benefits in Denmark, the Netherlands, the United Kingdom and the United States claim about one quarter of the economy's domestic production.

Accounting for (changing) tax systems can also give a better impression of social effort **over time**. For example, Danish reforms in 1994 meant that some pensions and social assistance benefits became taxable, while gross benefit payments were raised to preserve their net value. In all, gross public spending increased by about 2% of GDP from 1993 to 1995, while net social expenditure indicators were largely unaffected.

Status indicators: Income inequality (B2).
Response indicators: Tax wedge (A13), Public social expenditure (B6), Private social expenditure (B7).

B8. NET SOCIAL EXPENDITURE

Chart B8.1. **Social expenditure as a percentage of GDP for selected OECD countries, 1995**

- Gross expenditure
- Net expenditure
- Average gross expenditure
- Average net expenditure

Public social expenditure, 1995
Percentage of GDP at factor costs

Total social expenditure, 1995
Percentage of GDP at factor costs

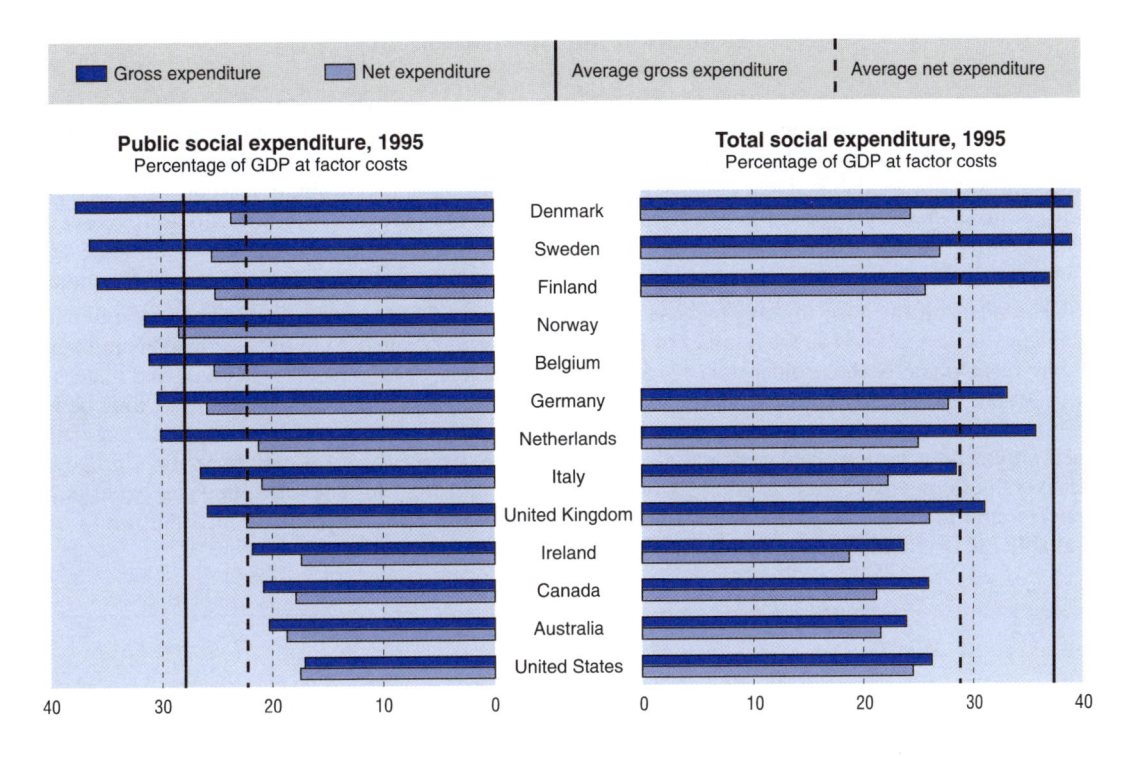

Countries (top to bottom): Denmark, Sweden, Finland, Norway, Belgium, Germany, Netherlands, Italy, United Kingdom, Ireland, Canada, Australia, United States

Table B8.1. **Net public social expenditure, 1995**

Per cent of GDP at factor costs

	Australia	Denmark	Germany	Netherlands	United Kingdom	United States
Item:						
1. Gross public social expenditure	20.3	37.6	30.4	30.1	25.9	17.1
− Direct taxes and social contributions paid on transfers	0.3	6.1	1.2	5.1	0.4	0.3
2. Net cash direct public social expenditure	20.0	31.5	29.2	25.0	25.5	16.8
− Indirect taxes	1.6	8.0	4.2	3.9	3.7	0.9
3. Net direct public social expenditure	18.4	23.5	25.0	21.1	21.7	15.9
+ TBSPs excluding TBSPs on pensions	0.3	0.1	0.9	0.1	0.6	1.5
4. Net current public social expenditure	18.7	23.6	25.9	21.2	22.3	17.5
Memorandum item:						
TBSPs on pensions	1.9		0.1	2.1	2.8	1.0

Source: Adema (1999).

Further reading

- Adema, W. (2001), "Eine vergleichende Analyse des Wohlfahrtstaates in ausgewählten OECD-Ländern", in E. Theurl (ed.), *Der Sozialstaat an der Jahrtausendwende*, Physica-Verlag, Heidelberg, Germany.
- Adema, W. (1999), "Net total social expenditure", Labour Market and Social Policy Occasional Paper, No. 39, OECD, Paris.
- Adema, W., M. Einerhand, B. Eklind, J. Lotz and M. Pearson (1996), "Net public social expenditure", Labour Market and Social Policy Occasional Paper, No. 19, OECD, Paris.
- OECD (2000), *OECD Social Expenditure Database, 1980-1997*, Paris.

B9. BENEFIT RECIPIENCY

Definition and measurement

The proportion of the population in receipt of social benefits provides a measure on the magnitude of a country's social protection system (B6), but it says little about the extent to which benefit-recipients depend on their benefit as their main source of (family) income (A4). Information on benefit-dependency is not available across countries on a comparable basis for two main reasons. First, point-in-time estimates make it impossible to determine whether an individual of working age will receive the benefit during the rest of the year. Second, individuals can receive different benefits at the same time, complicating the assessment of dependency on benefit income for that individual, let alone household.

The position of those in retirement is treated elsewhere (A6). Hence, the indicator on benefit-recipiency is here defined as the number of benefit years for those aged 15 to 65 *vis-à-vis* the number of employment years for those older than 15, not including benefit years related to sickness and maternity. Both benefit and employment are denoted in full-time equivalents so as to account for part-time benefit receipt and part-time employment. Benefits covered in the calculation include those regarding unemployment; long-term sickness and disability; social assistance; lone-parent benefits; old age and survivors pensions (to recipients younger than 65), and maternity. Child benefits, housing benefits, tax benefits and medical insurance benefits are not included (B8). Comparative information is only available for 11 countries as studied by the Netherlands Economic Institute.

Evidence and explanations

In most countries **trends** in benefit recipiency ratios reflect business-cycle trends to some extent, and most clearly in Sweden, Spain, the United Kingdom and the United States (Chart B9.1). However, differences in trends across countries do not merely reflect fluctuations in take-up of unemployment and social assistance benefits. The huge variation in benefit recipiency ratios between Austria, Belgium, Denmark, France and Germany on the one hand and Spain and the Unites States on the other is related to whether or not a considerable proportion of the working age population has access to "other" social protection programmes.

In comparison to Japan, Spain and the United States, western and northern European social protection systems have allowed for individuals of working age to use retirement, early retirement and disability programmes to detach themselves from the labour market. In recent years policy reforms have focussed on reducing the use of such labour market withdrawal benefits, while young people's access to social programmes has often also been restricted (A3). The economic upswing in the late 1990s further contributed to a stabilisation or reduction of benefit-recipiency ratios in most countries, except Germany and Japan.

Those not in receipt of benefit income are more likely to work in Japan and the United States (with a high incidence of low-paid employment, B3), than in Spain, where the proportion of the working-age population that depends on others (spouses, extended family networks) for their income is 45% (Table B9.1). This proportion is still close to 30% in the Netherlands, despite the increase in female employment (A1).

Status indicators: Employment (A1), Unemployment (A2), Jobless youth (A3), Jobless households (A4), Retirement ages (A6), Low paid employment (B3).
Response indicators: Public social expenditure (B6), Net social expenditure (B8).

B9. BENEFIT RECIPIENCY

Chart B9.1. **Benefit recipiency ratio for the working age population (15-64), 1980-1998**

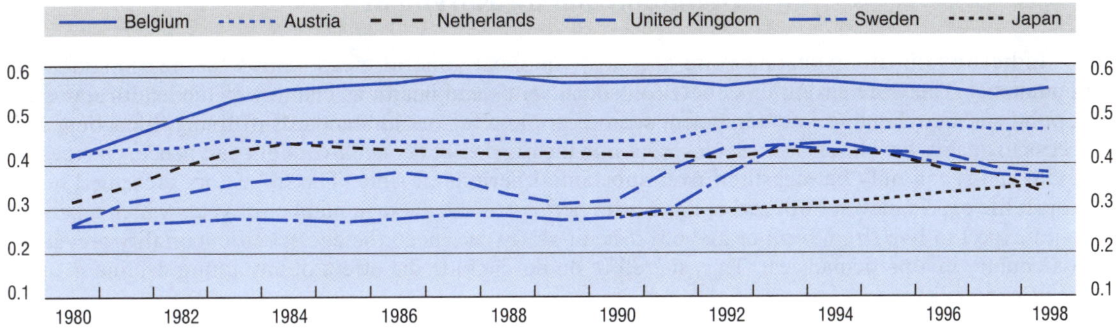

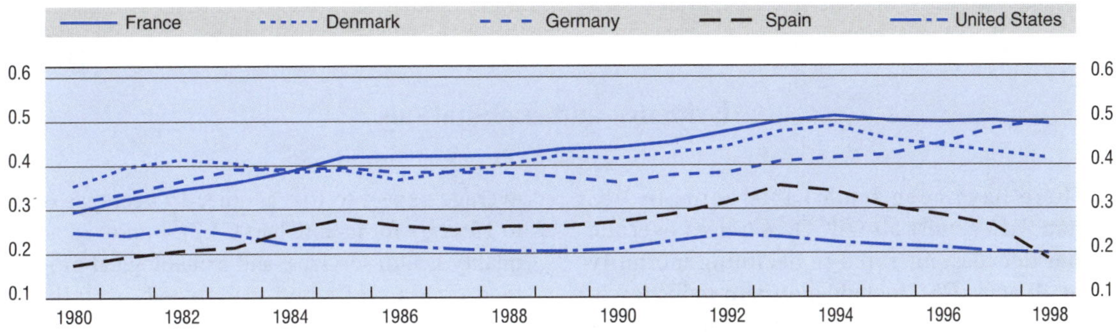

Table B9.1. **Distribution of the working age population by employment and recipiency status, 1980 and 1998**

	Employment 1980 (1990 for Japan)	Employment 1998	Benefit recipients 1980 (1990 for Japan)	Benefit recipients 1998	No benefit, no work 1980 (1990 for Japan)	No benefit, no work 1998	Benefit recipiency ratio 1980 (1990 for Japan)	Benefit recipiency ratio 1998
Spain	0.48	0.47	0.08	0.09	0.43	0.45	0.17	0.19
United States	0.60	0.66	0.15	0.13	0.25	0.20	0.25	0.20
Netherlands	0.50	0.54	0.16	0.18	0.35	0.28	0.32	0.33
Japan	0.68	0.68	0.19	0.24	0.13	0.08	0.29	0.35
Sweden	0.63	0.55	0.16	0.20	0.21	0.25	0.26	0.37
Great Britain	0.60	0.58	0.16	0.22	0.24	0.19	0.27	0.38
Denmark	0.59	0.61	0.21	0.25	0.21	0.14	0.35	0.42
Austria	0.55	0.56	0.23	0.27	0.22	0.16	0.43	0.48
France	0.59	0.52	0.17	0.26	0.24	0.22	0.29	0.49
Germany	0.58	0.53	0.18	0.27	0.23	0.20	0.32	0.50
Belgium	0.54	0.52	0.23	0.30	0.23	0.18	0.42	0.57

Source: NEI (2000).

Further reading

■ OECD (1999), *A Caring World: The New Social Policy Agenda*, Paris. ■ NEI (2000), *Benefit Dependency Ratios: An Analysis of Nine European Countries, Japan and the US*, Netherlands Economic Institute, Elsevier, The Netherlands. ■ Einerhand, M., I. Eriksson and M. van Leuvensteijn (2000), "Benefit Dependency and the Dynamics of the Welfare State", *International Social Security Review*, No. 2001/01.

C1. LIFE EXPECTANCY

Definition and measurement

Indicators on life expectancy are arguably the most general measures on the health status of populations. There are strong links between social status and health as changes in the health status of populations are related to interdependent socio-economic factors as standards of living, lifestyles, and access to quality health services. Socio-economic factors do not change overnight and hence, changes in health status can only be measured over substantial periods of time. The indicators presented here, project life expectancy at birth and at age 65 are defined as the average number of years which a person could expect to live (from birth or age 65) if he or she experienced the age-specific mortality prevalent in a country in a particular year. They therefore do not include the effect of any future decline in age-specific mortality rates.

Evidence and explanations

There have been remarkable gains in life expectancy in almost all OECD countries over the last four decades, mirrored in declining mortality rates at all ages (C5), including a sharp reduction in infant mortality rates (C2) and higher survival rates at older ages (C3). On average, **life expectancy at birth** across OECD countries has increased from 65.7 to 73.3 years for men and from 70.8 to 79.5 years for women (Chart C1.1). In 1998, life expectancy at birth was highest in Japan, at 77.2 years for men and 84 years for women. Although the gains in life span were not uniform across countries, there has been convergence towards the OECD average, particularly for countries (*e.g.* Korea, Mexico and Turkey) with low life expectancy at birth in 1960 (see the annex on Internet). Some Eastern European countries have experienced much lower gains in life expectancy in recent years. In Hungary, for example, the relative stability in the low male life expectancy has been attributed to unhealthy lifestyles, poor diets, and excessive alcohol and tobacco consumption (OECD, 1999).

Life expectancy at age 65 has actually increased faster since 1980 than over the 1960s and 1970s (see the annex on Internet). By 1998, women at age 65 in OECD countries could on average expect to live another 19 years, as opposed to 15 years for men (Chart C1.2). Improved access to quality health services, and technological progress in medicine as reflected in reduced mortality from cardiovascular diseases have also contributed to increased life expectancy at age 65 (AIHW, 1998; WHO and Ministero della Sanità Repubblica Italiana, 1999). The quality of life of elderly persons seems also to have increased in most OECD countries (C4).

Over the past forty years, life expectancy increased for both sexes, but these gains have generally been greater for women (8½ extra years at birth; 4 extra years at age 65) than for men (7½ extra years at birth; 2½ at age 65). Hence, the **gender gap in longevity** between male and female life expectancy has widened. Life expectancy for both sexes is highest in Japan, but for men the countries which follow in rank are Switzerland and Iceland. For women the countries which follow are France, Switzerland, Spain and Italy.

Status indicators: Infant mortality (C2), Potential years of life lost (C3), Disability-free life expectancy (C4), Accidents (C5).
Response indicators: Health care expenditure (C7), Health infrastructure (C9).

C1. LIFE EXPECTANCY

Chart C1.1. **Trends in life expectancy at birth for selected countries (1960-1998)**

Chart C1.2. **Life expectancy at 65 years old, most recent years in 1990s**

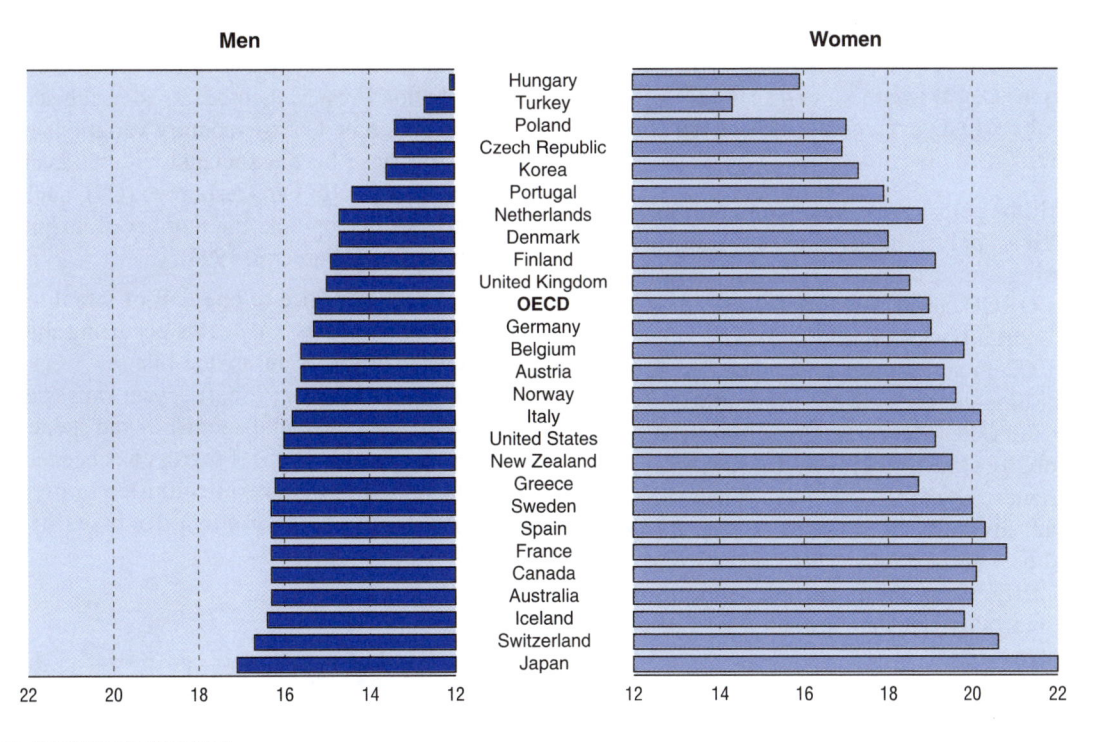

Source: OECD Health Data 2000.

Further reading

■ OECD (1999), *OECD Economic Surveys: Hungary 1999*, Paris. ■ Australian Institute of Health and Welfare (1998), *Australia's Health 1998*, Canberra. ■ World Health Organisation and Ministero della Sanità Repubblica Italiana (1999), *Health in Italy in the 21st Century*.

C2. INFANT MORTALITY

Definition and measurement

Infant mortality rates are one of the most widely used indicators in international comparisons to judge the effect on human health of general technological, economic and social conditions. Infant mortality is defined as the number of deaths of children under one year of age per 1 000 live births.

Evidence and explanations

Over the last four decades, infant mortality has **declined significantly** in all OECD countries (Chart C2.1). For the 22 countries for which data are available for 1960 to 1998, average mortality rates declined from on average 39.7 deaths per 1 000 live births in 1960 to 7.4 in 1998. The decline in infant mortality has been most pronounced in Portugal: from 78 deaths per 1 000 children in 1960 – twice as high as the OECD average – to 6 per 1 000 by 1998 – below the OECD average of 7.4 (see the annex on Internet).

Although progress has been achieved in all countries, and disparities across countries are narrowing, infant mortality rates vary considerably **across OECD countries**. In 1998, the incidence of infant mortality was highest in Turkey and Mexico (Chart C2.1) and lowest in Iceland, Sweden and Japan. Some countries with infant mortality rates below the OECD average (for example, Finland, Greece, Iceland, Ireland, Luxembourg, the Netherlands and the UK) reported an annual increase in infant mortality in at least one year during the second part of the 1990s. This suggests that it may prove difficult to obtain further reductions once infant mortality rates are around 4 to 5 deaths per 1 000 live births.

Infant mortality is related to **average income levels** across countries: richer countries have lower infant mortality rates than poorer countries as illustrated in Chart C2.2. Given comparable income levels, countries with a more equal income distribution (B2) tend to have lower infant mortality rates than countries with larger income dispersion (Hales *et al.*, 1999). But it is unclear whether relative poverty (B1) *per se* is related to higher infant mortality, or whether infant mortality is higher among families at the bottom end of the income distribution because their access to health services is relatively limited. Cross-country variations in infant mortality have been associated with the availability of specific health care resources (C9), such as the number of doctors and the number of hospital beds (Grubaugh and Santerre, 1994).

About one-third to one-half of infant mortality in OECD countries are deaths occurring during the first week of life or during the first few weeks. After the first few weeks of life, the main **causes** of infant mortality are congenital anomalies and sudden infant death syndrome (SIDS). Progress has been achieved in recent years in several countries in preventing deaths from these important causes of infant mortality.

Status indicators: Relative poverty (B1), Income inequality (B2), Life expectancy (C1), Potential years of life lost (C3).
Response indicators: Health care expenditure (C7), Health infrastructure (C9).

C2. INFANT MORTALITY

Chart C2.1. **Infant mortality, 1960-latest 1990s**

Chart C2.2. **Infant mortality in OECD countries related to income, latest 1990s**

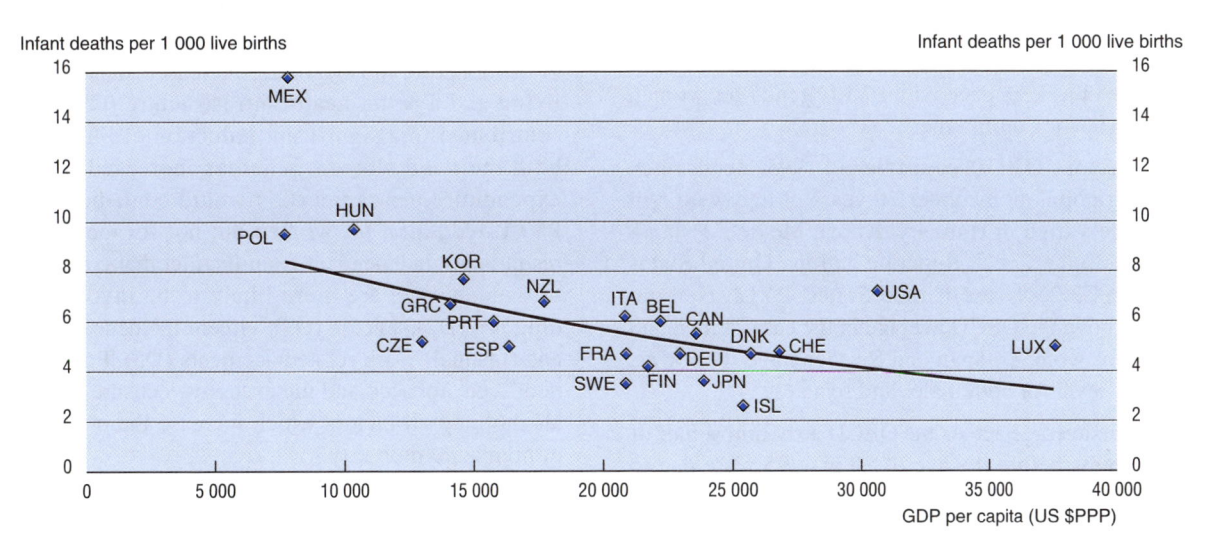

Source: OECD Health Data 2000.

Further reading

- Grubaugh, S.G. and R.E. Santerre (1994), "Comparing the performance of health care systems: An alternative approach", *Southern Economic Journal*, 60, pp. 1030-1042. ■ Hales, S., P. Howden-Chapman, C. Salmond, A. Woodward and J. Mackenbach (1999), "National infant mortality rates in relation to gross national product and distribution of income", *The Lancet*, Vol. 353, December 11, 1999, p. 2047.

C3. POTENTIAL YEARS OF LIFE LOST

Definition and measurement

It is in the poorer countries, the most disadvantaged groups in society (B1), and those with the least education (A10) that the greatest concentration of morbidity is found and, often, the shortest longevity. Indicators on premature mortality are important as they help identify fatalities which could be potentially avoided by (amongst other things), better access to quality social and health services. Premature mortality is here defined as death before the age of 70. Potential years of life lost (PYLL) is measured by adding up age-specific death rates that are weighted by the difference between age 70 and the age in question. For example, a death at 5 years of age is counted as 65 years of PYLL. The indicator is expressed per 100 000 females and males. Trends in PYLL can differ from those in life expectancy (C1) because they give greater weight to mortality at an early age.

Evidence and explanations

Given **trends** in infant mortality and life expectancy over the last four decades, it is not surprising that premature mortality, measured in terms of potential years of life lost (PYLL), has on average more than halved across OECD countries (Chart C3.1). The decline in PYLL has been particularly strong for women during the 1960s, 1970s and 1980s, but since 1990 the decline in PYLL for men has kept pace with PYLL trends for women (see the annex on Internet).

Across **OECD countries** in 1995, death rates among populations under 70 years of age were still relatively high in Hungary, Korea, Mexico, Poland, Portugal, the Czech Republic and the United States (Chart C3.2). In the United States, PYLL is about 20% above the OECD average in the case of men and 11% for women. Japan and Sweden have the lowest PYLL-level for both males and females.

On average across the OECD area almost half of the deaths before the age of 70 in 1995 were due to cancers and external causes, including accidents (C5). **Reasons for premature mortality** vary significantly across the sexes. For women, the main causes of death before the age of 70 were cancers (31%), followed by external causes (16%), and circulatory diseases, including heart attacks (15%). External factors such as accidents and violence were the most frequent cause of death among men before the age of 70 (27%), followed by cancers (20%) and circulatory diseases (20%).

Or (2000) provides evidence on basis of the comprehensive information-set available in *OECD Health Data 2000,* that both **social** and **medical** factors need to be considered to explain the incidence of death before the age of 70. Increased standards of living and a better health infrastructure (C9) have contributed to a significant reduction of PYLL for both men and women, whereas increased health expenditure per capita (C7) would contribute to a PYLL-reduction for women but not for men. This result is not independent from the fact that compared to women, men are more likely to be involved in drug use (D2), suicide (D3), violent incidences (D4), and (manual) work-related accidents (D5). Pollution, poor diets, tobacco and the excessive consumption of alcohol, are all factors which increase the incidence of premature mortality.

Status indicators: Relative poverty (B1), Life expectancy (C1), Infant mortality (C2), Drug use and related deaths (D2), Suicide (D3), Crime (D4). **Response indicators**: Educational attainment (A10), Health care expenditure (C7), Health infrastructure (C9).

C3. POTENTIAL YEARS OF LIFE LOST

Chart C3.1. **Trends in potential years of life lost by gender**
In thousands of premature deaths

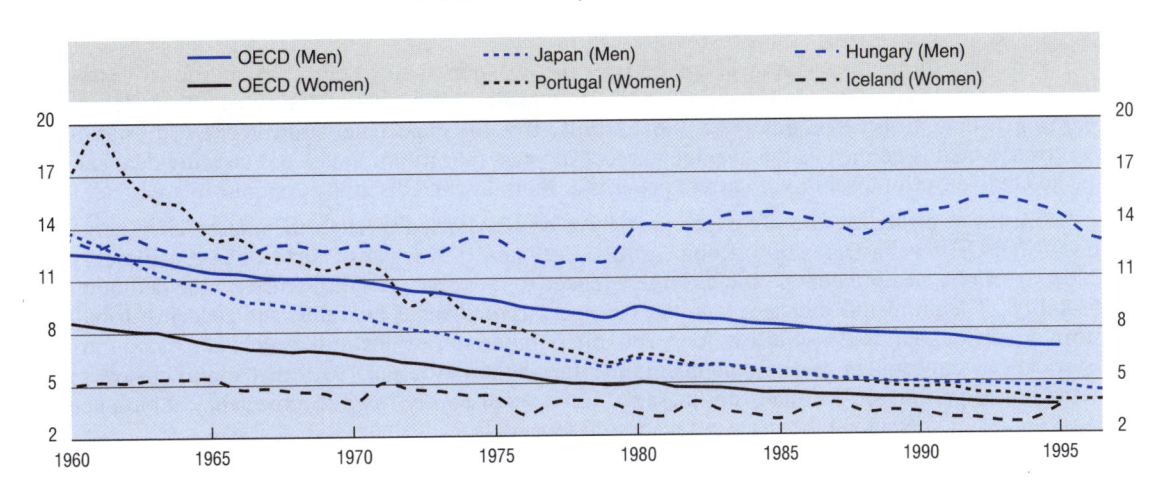

Chart C3.2. **Potential years of life lost by gender, 1995**
In thousands of premature deaths

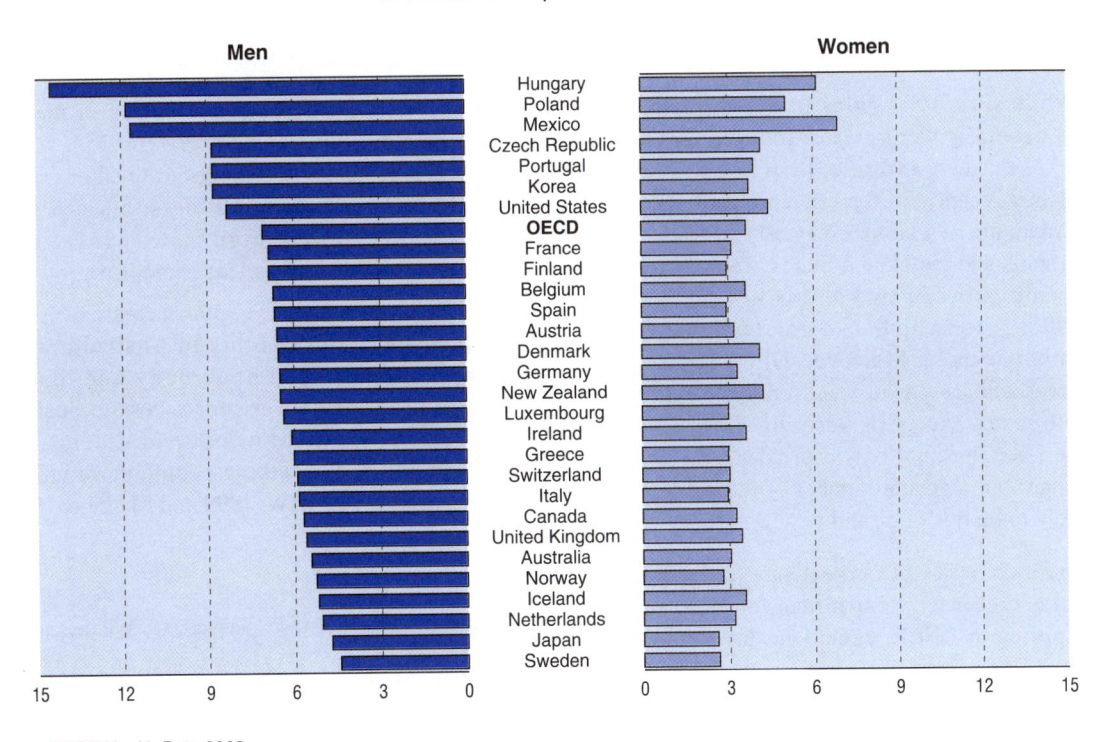

Source: OECD Health Data 2000.

Further reading

- Or, Z. (2000), "Determinants of health outcomes in industrialised countries: A pooled, cross-country, time series analysis ", *OECD Economic studies*, No. 30, pp. 53-78.

C4. DISABILITY-FREE LIFE EXPECTANCY

Definition and measurement

The increase in life expectancy at age 65 begs the question as to whether the additional years are extending the independent life-course, or leading to a prolonged period of frailty and dependency. In order to get some measure on this issue, the disability-free life expectancy indicator (DFLE) has been developed, which is defined as the average number of years (at birth or at age 65) an individual can be expected to live free of disability if current patterns of mortality and disability continue to apply (C1).

Estimates of disability-free life expectancy have been collected through the international network REVES (OECD Health Data 2000; Robine *et al.*, 1998 and 1999). These survey-based estimates are subject to serious measurement problems largely related to cross-national differences in the definition of "disability". Therefore, this indicator facilitates an analysis of changes over time and gender distribution within countries, but does not allow for a reliable comparison of absolute levels across countries. Historical data concern two separate points in time during the 1980s and 1990s that approximately span a 10-year time period (see the annex on Internet). Trends in disability-free life expectancy at birth and at age 65 are rather similar and therefore not discussed separately.

Evidence and explanations

While since 1960 **gains in life expectancy** at age 65 generally were greater for women than for men (C1), the gender gap in longevity has diminished recently in the few countries for which DFLE-data are available, especially in Canada, the Netherlands and the United States (Table C4.1). For the period between two points in time – 1980s and 1990s – for which data are available, DFLE generally increased. Moreover, DFLE at the age of 65 increased at least as fast as overall life expectancy for both sexes, except in Australia, Japan, Norway and the UK. Thus, not only can older now expect to live longer but a greater number of these extra years are likely to be free of disability.

In all countries life expectancy (at birth and at age 65) is higher for **women** than for **men**, and this also applies to DFLE, except in the Netherlands (Chart C4.1). Despite the incompatibility of disability definitions, it seems generally true that although women live longer than men (C1), they tend to live a (slightly) greater proportion of their lives with some disability (*OECD Health Data 2000*). In part this is related to the longer survival of women in the aftermath of chronic illness, but can also be related to relatively high male involvement in accidents, suicide and violent crime (C3).

The reasons underlying the increase over time in the prevalence of disability in **Australia** include: changes in survey methodology and disability support programmes, greater access to health care professionals and knowledge of diagnosis, and changing attitudes making people more willing to report disability (AIHW, 1999 and Mathers, 1996).

Status indicators: Life expectancy (C1), Potential years of life lost (C3).
Response indicators: Benefit recipiency (B9), Older people in institutions (C6), Health care expenditure (C7).

C4. DISABILITY-FREE LIFE EXPECTANCY

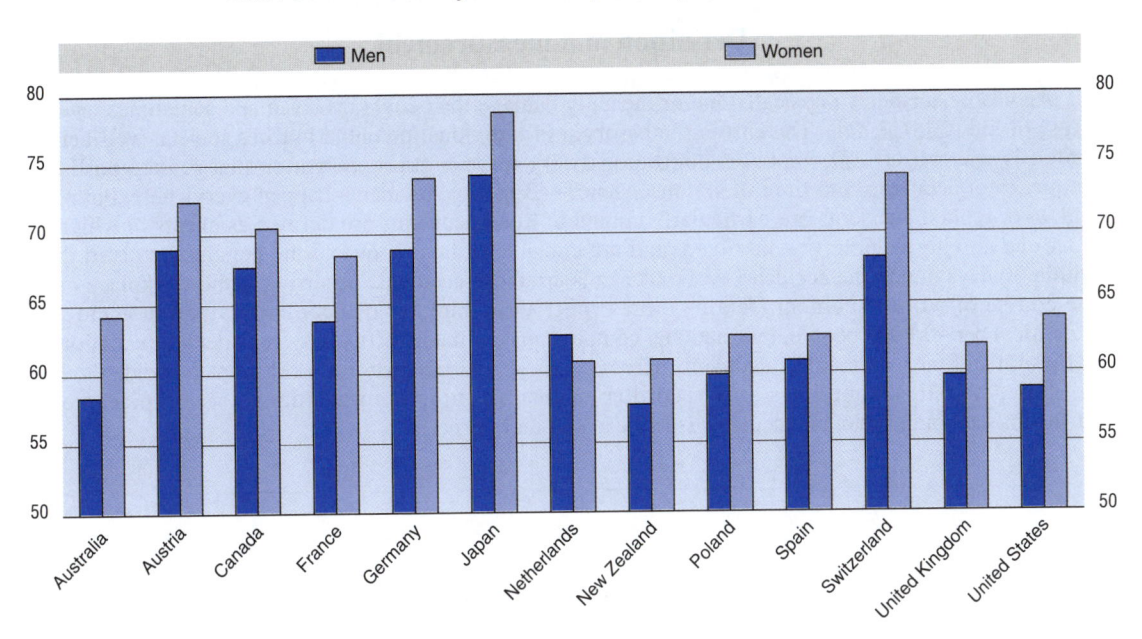

Chart C4.1. **Disability-free life expectancy at birth in the 1990s**

Table C4.1. **Percentage point change per year in disability-free life expectancy at age 65 between the 1980s and the 1990s**

	Men		Women	
	Life expectancy	Disability-free life expectancy	Life expectancy	Disability-free life expectancy
Australia	1.0	−1.6	0.6	−0.8
United Kingdom	0.8	0.0	0.6	0.9
Norway	0.2	0.4	0.6	0.2
Switzerland	0.7	0.7	0.8	2.0
United States	0.7	0.8	0.3	0.5
Japan	1.0	1.2	1.2	0.9
France	1.1	1.4	0.9	2.1
Finland	1.1	1.5	0.8	1.1
Germany	0.7	1.6	0.6	1.5
Canada	1.0	1.8	0.5	1.4
Netherlands	0.5	1.9	0.1	1.5
Korea	1.1	4.1	0.6	4.7

Source: OECD Health Data 2000.

Further reading
- Australian Institute of Health and Welfare (1999), *Australia's Welfare 1999*, Canberra. - Mathers, C. (1996), "Trends in health expectancies in Australia 1981-1993", *Journal of the Australian Population Association*, 13(1), pp. 1-16. - Robine, J-M, I. Romieu and E. Cambois (1999), "Health expectancy indicators", *Bulletin of the World Health Organization*, 77 (2), pp. 181-185. - Robine, J-M, I. Romieu and M. Jee (1998), "Health expectancies in OECD countries", REVES Paper No. 317.

© OECD 2001

C5. ACCIDENTS

Definition and measurement

Avoidable accidents physically and/or mentally damage the people involved and sometimes lead to a loss of life (C1, C3, C4). The ensuing impairment of individual potential reduces societal well-being, which is why all OECD countries continuously try to strengthen measures that reduce both the frequency of accidents and limit their consequences (B6, C7). Accidents happen everywhere, but road and work-related accidents are particularly common. Road accidents are defined as events in which at least one moving vehicle was involved, and are considered fatal if one of the persons involved died within 30 days due to the accident. Work accidents are those accidents occurring at the workplace or in the course of work. Accident (fatality) rates specify the number of people involved in accidents (fatalities) per 100 000 people. International comparisons are made difficult by considerable variation in definition and measurement of accidents across countries, particularly for work-related accidents. For example, statistics sometimes only record compensated injuries or accidents in workplaces of a sufficient size, rather than all accidents (see the annex on Internet).

Evidence and explanations

Ideally, no accidents happen at all, but failing that, the accident rates should be as low as possible. A safe and healthy living and working environment engenders low accident rates, as measured against the population. But these accident rates should also be considered in the **context** of employment levels and vehicle density. For example, while the road-accident rate in the United States is 6 times that recorded for Turkey (Chart C5.1), the Turkish road-accident fatality rate measured against the number of cars is 9 times higher than in the US. Similarly, cross-country differences in climate, vehicle characteristics, and the length of the road network and its characteristics affect accident rates, but their roles are difficult to measure. These factors also make it impossible to use accident rates for international comparisons of the propensity of citizens to adhere to societal norms (D7), which are likely to affect the frequency (and intensity) with which accidents occur.

Road accident related fatality rates have decreased everywhere during the 1990s, except in Ireland (see the annex on Internet), while trends in casualty rates vary across the OECD (Chart C5.1). So even if road accidents happen more often, their occurrence is less likely to lead to fatalities. Tightening of drink-driving regulations and their enforcement, awareness campaigns and improved vehicle safety-features tend to reduce casualty rates, while increasing vehicle density pushes casualty rates up. Once pedestrians are involved in road accidents they are more likely to suffer fatal injuries than any other road-user (Table C5.1).

Although about 45% of the population is in work across the OECD area, fatal work-accidents occur far less often than fatal road accidents. Trends in **work-accidents** have generally stabilised or declined since the end of the 1980s. The frequency of fatal accidents increases with age, except in Greece and Spain (ILO, 2000). Accident rates vary across industries, and are most concentrated in the construction, transport, agriculture and fishing industries (Table C5.2). Since most workers in these sectors are men, they are more likely to be involved in accidents.

Status indicators: Life expectancy (C1), Potential years of life lost (C3), Disability-free life expectancy (C4).
Response indicators: Public social expenditure (B6), Health care expenditure (C7), Prisoners (D7).

C5. ACCIDENTS

Chart C5.1. **Road traffic accidents: people injured and killed per 100 000 population, 1980-1998**

Fatality rates in brackets, 1998

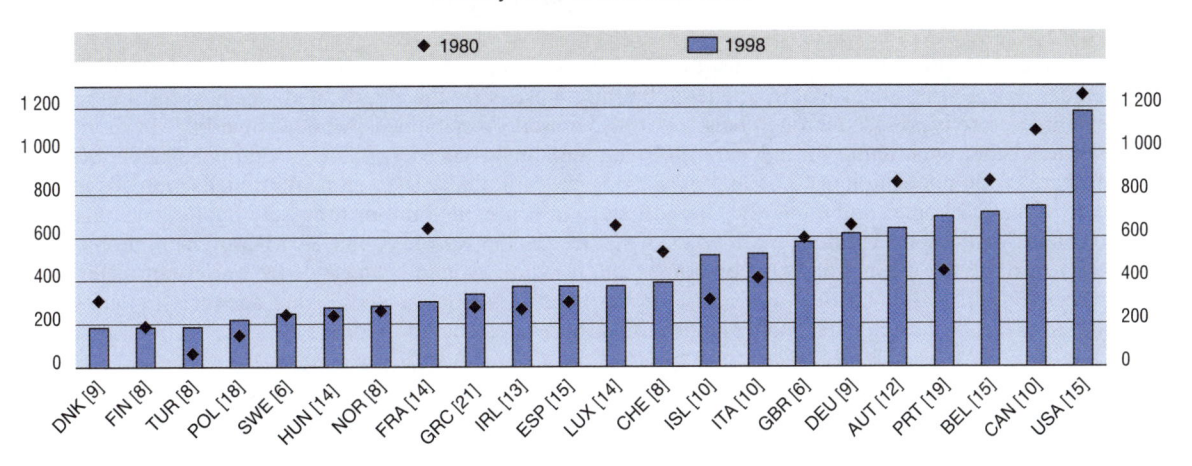

[Bar chart showing 1980 (diamonds) and 1998 (bars) data for: DNK [9], FIN [8], TUR [8], POL [18], SWE [6], HUN [14], NOR [8], FRA [14], GRC [21], IRL [13], ESP [15], LUX [14], CHE [8], ISL [10], ITA [10], GBR [6], DEU [9], AUT [12], PRT [19], BEL [15], CAN [10], USA [15]]

Source: ECMT (2000a) and UN (1999, 2000).

Table C5.1. **Fatal road accidents by user category per 1 000 casualties (1995)**

	Pedestrian	On bicycle	On motorcycle	Car driver	Car passenger		Pedestrian	On bicycle	On motorcycle	Car driver	Car passenger
United Kingdom	22	8	21	9	9	New Zealand	61	17	38	30	35
Germany	28	9	24	19	16	Czech Republic	63	34	30	42	31
Canada	31	7	25	11	11	Finland	66	32	39	48	29
Austria	34	14	30	20	18	Turkey	68	44	32	48	42
Switzerland	38	14	26	23	19	Spain	69	39	37	47	38
Belgium	38	17	33	22	15	Denmark	71	39	44	55	49
Norway	47	7	17	22	16	Hungary	96	67	36	47	35
Portugal	47	37	39	30	24	Netherlands	102	85	88	113	92
Sweden	48	16	48	24	22	Poland	104	94	79	83	57
France	48	42	43	54	43						
Italy	56	41	30	21	18						

Source: ECMT (2000).

Table C5.2. **Fatal work-related accidents per 100 000 workers (late 1990s)**

	Average	Agr-Fish	Construction	Transport		Average	Agr-Fish	Construction	Transport
Reported injuries					*Compensated injuries*				
United Kingdom	1.0	11.1	6.7	2.0	Finland	2.7	2.6	6.5	11.7
Iceland	1.7	15.9	0.0	0.0	Switzerland	3.2		10.7	10.4
Sweden	2.5	50.0	7.1	4.3	Belgium	4.0	0.0	19.5	8.2
Norway	3.1	38.9	12.3	6.4	Australia	4.2		8.6	10.7
Denmark	3.2	25.8	9.0	7.7	Canada	7.3	32.1	31.4	13.2
Ireland	4.4	95.7	18.8	11.7	Italy	8.7	32.2	27.5	20.2
Czech Republic	5.7	9.8	8.8	3.7					
Hungary	5.9	10.7	39.7	8.4					
Poland	6.0	9.8	16.5	8.9					
Portugal	7.0	17.4	31.3	11.8					
Mexico	7.2	1.9	17.8	16.9					
Spain	11.0	28.5	28.5	29.4					

Source: ILO (2000).

Further reading

■ ECMT (2000), *Trends in the Transport Sector*, European Conference of Ministers of Transport, Paris. ■ ECMT (2000a), *Statistical Report on Road Accidents 1995-96*, European Conference of Ministers of Transport, Paris. ■ ILO (2000), *Yearbook of Labour Statistics 1999*, International Labour Office, Geneva. ■ UN (1999), *World Population Prospects: the 1998 revision*, New York. ■ UN (2000), *Statistics of Road Traffic Accidents in Europe and North America*, New York.

C6. OLDER PEOPLE IN INSTITUTIONS

Definition and measurement

The concept of older people in institutions covers a range of settings varying with the intensity of medical services that are available: sheltered housing, hostels for the elderly, and "medical institutions". Sometimes, care is provided through long-term stays in acute hospital beds, while "home-like" institutions provide a better opportunity for independent living until an advanced age. The institutionalisation rate is the share of the population aged 65 and over living in institutions. Data on institutionalisation covers a range of staffed homes, including the share of stays in acute, medium or long-stay public hospitals or psychiatric institutions, but not certain types of service flats in Nordic countries. Measurement problems exist regarding the distinction between homes and institutions, and because of the variety of different sources for national data (local and central governments, health and social care agencies), making it difficult to collate data on older people in institutions on a cross-country basis.

Evidence and explanations

Institutionalisation rates vary **across countries** (Chart C6.1). The share of the elderly population living in institutions is relatively high in the Netherlands and Sweden at over 8%, while in southern European countries institutionalisation rates are below 4%. Cross-country differences in institutionalisation rates cannot be attributed to differences in the prevalence of disability (C4).

In most OECD countries, trends reveal that elderly persons increasingly live on their own. Since they live longer (C1), this is particularly true of women (Chart C6.2). In all countries for which data are available, institutionalisation rates for elderly up to 80 years of age declined between the mid-1980s and the mid-1990s (Table C6.1). This tendency towards "de-institutionalisation" is related to sometimes interdependent factors which include: increased reluctance among the elderly to enter institutions; the high costs of institutional care (B6, C7); and, a policy shift emphasising "independent living". Another factor was stigma attached to being in care services provided within a social assistance framework.

As a result, **alternative forms of housing/care** have been developed, although a full continuum of care services is often not available in many places in all countries. While the share of the more medically oriented care institutions has certainly reduced, other forms of sheltered housing have often been promoted and developed. Often newly developed institutions provide older persons with alternative housing arrangements, as for example in the Nordic countries.

The proportion of elderly persons living within the **extended family environment** is diminishing, although it remains comparatively high in Japan, Korea and Southern Europe. Even when cohabitation does not prevail, (extended) family-members provide the bulk of care as informal caregivers.

Status indicators: Life expectancy (C1), Disability-free life expectancy (C4).
Response indicators: Public social expenditure (B6), Health care expenditure (C7).

C6. OLDER PEOPLE IN INSTITUTIONS

Chart C6.1. **Share of population aged 65 and over in institutions (mid-1990s)**

Chart C6.2. **Share of older persons living alone (1970-1996)**

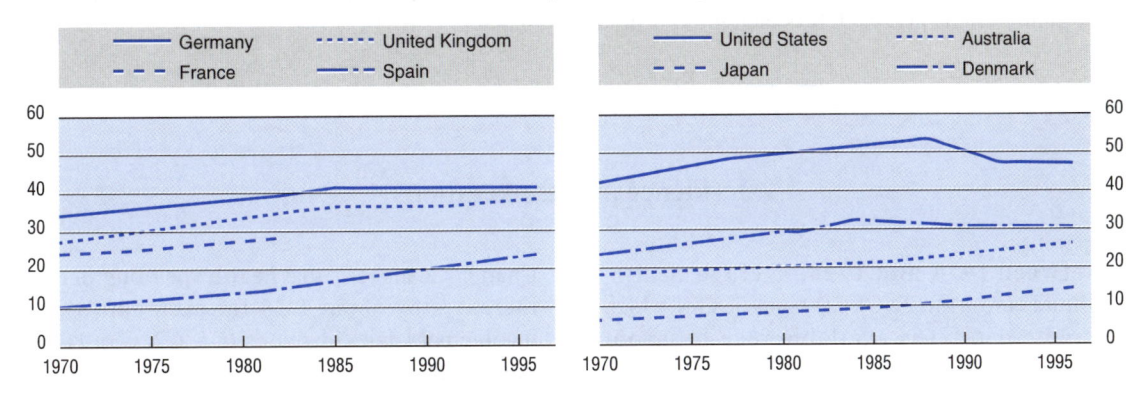

Source: Jacobzone (1999).

Table C6.1. **Trends in institutionalisation rates**

Per cent of the population in long-term care institutions by age groups

	Year	65-69	70-74	75-79	over 80
Australia	1993	←	1.8	→	17.6
	Annual change (1985 to 1993)	←	6.0	→	–4.3
Canada	1991	1.4	2.4	5.6	23.4
	Annual change (1986 to 1991)	–4.2	–2.5	–1.1	–0.2
France	1991	1.2	2.0	4.8	17.0
	Annual change (1981 to 1991)	–4.0	–4.7	–9.0	6.0
Sweden	1995	←	3.1	→	25.1
	Annual change (1980 to 1995)	←	1.0	→	–0.5
United States	1994	0.9	1.8	3.8	15.3
	Annual change (1982 to 1994)	–2.9	–1.9	–2.2	–1.2

Source: Jacobzone *et al.* (1998).

Further reading

- Jacobzone, S. (1999), "Ageing and care for frail elderly persons: An overview of international perspectives", Labour Market and Social Policy Occasional Papers, No. 38, OECD, Paris. ■ Jacobzone S., E. Cambois, E. Chaplain and J.M. Robine (1998), "The health of older persons in OECD countries: Is it improving fast enough to compensate for population ageing?", Labour Market and Social Policy Occasional Papers, No. 37, OECD, Paris. ■ Jenson, J. and S. Jacobzone (2000), "Care allowances for the frail elderly and their impact on women caregivers' perspectives", Labour Market and Social Policy Occasional Papers, No. 41, OECD, Paris. ■ OECD (1998), *Maintaining Prosperity in an Ageing Society*, Paris.

C7. HEALTH CARE EXPENDITURE

Definition and measurement

Total expenditure on health is the amount spent on health care goods and services plus capital investment in health care infrastructure. This includes outlays by both public and private sources (including households) on medical services provided by hospitals, nursing homes, outpatient facilities, ambulance services, home health care providers, laboratories, pharmacies and other retailers of therapeutic goods. Outlays on public health administration and prevention programmes are also included.

OECD Health Data 2000 includes comprehensive health expenditure estimates based on National health accounts that are in compliance with the recently developed System of Health Accounts (SHA) for 12 countries (OECD, 2000): Australia, Canada, Czech Republic, Denmark, Finland, France, Germany, Iceland, Korea, the Netherlands, New Zealand, and the US. For other countries, spending estimates are based on health spending as reported in the National Accounts. Measurement problems exist in that Austria, Sweden, and the UK draw the boundary between health and social care differently than elsewhere, thus reducing health spending relative to other countries. Private health expenditure for Belgium, Ireland and the UK is thought to be underestimated.

Evidence and explanations

Between 1970 and 1998, average health expenditure across the 22 OECD countries for which a complete dataset is available rose by about 3 percentage points to almost 8% of GDP (Chart C7.1). Health expenditure increases were particularly pronounced in the 1970s. As on average 75% of health expenditure is publicly financed (C8), the rise in health spending contributed to fiscal concerns in many OECD countries (A13). OECD (1992 and 1994) discussed a variety of cost-containment measures including the adoption of global budgets by public insurers. The introduction of such measures and the ascendancy of managed care in the United States seem to have had some success in curtailing the growth of health expenditure which since the beginning of the 1990s has been more or less in line with the growth rate of economies (Chart C7.1).

There are considerable cross-country differences in health care spending. Among OECD countries, Turkey and the United States had respectively, the lowest (4%) and highest (13.6%) level of health expenditure as a share of GDP (Chart C7.3). Relatively wealthy people and countries spend a higher proportion of total income on health care than relatively poor people and countries (OECD, 1999).

Chart C7.2 suggests that **health spending per capita** increases by about 1.26 for each unit by which income per capita increases (C1, C2, C3). However, this result includes both a volume and price effect, and as health services are labour intensive, there is a tendency for the relative price of health care to rise in response to standards of living across countries using similar health technology.

Cross-country differences in health care spending are also related to institutional variation in health care provision (C9). Such institutional variation covers many factors. For example, the extent to which systems rely on private sector provision; the role of general practitioners as gatekeepers in national health systems; the relative importance of medical care provided within hospitals, and the extent to which pharmaceutical products are being prescribed (see the annex on Internet).

Status indicators: Life expectancy (C1), Infant mortality (C2), Potential years of life lost (C3).
Response indicators: Tax wedge (A13), Responsibility for financing health care (C8), Health infrastructure (C9).

C7. HEALTH CARE EXPENDITURE

Chart C7.1. **Health care expenditure, 1970-1998**
Per cent of GDP

Chart C7.2. **Health expenditure and income per capita, 1998 (logarithmic scale)**

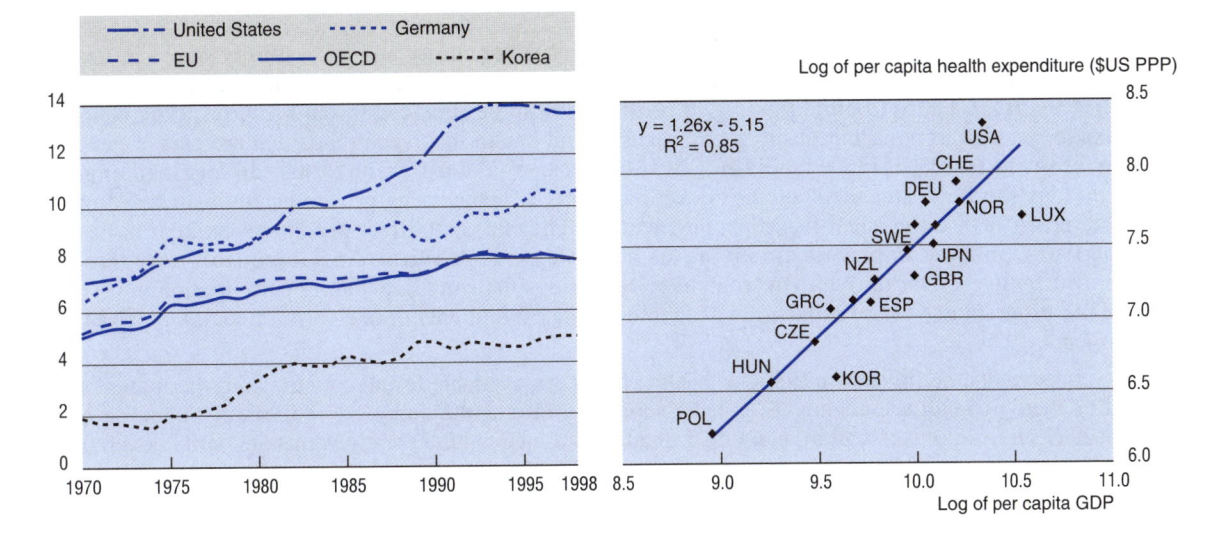

Chart C7.3. **Health care spending as a percentage of GDP, 1998**

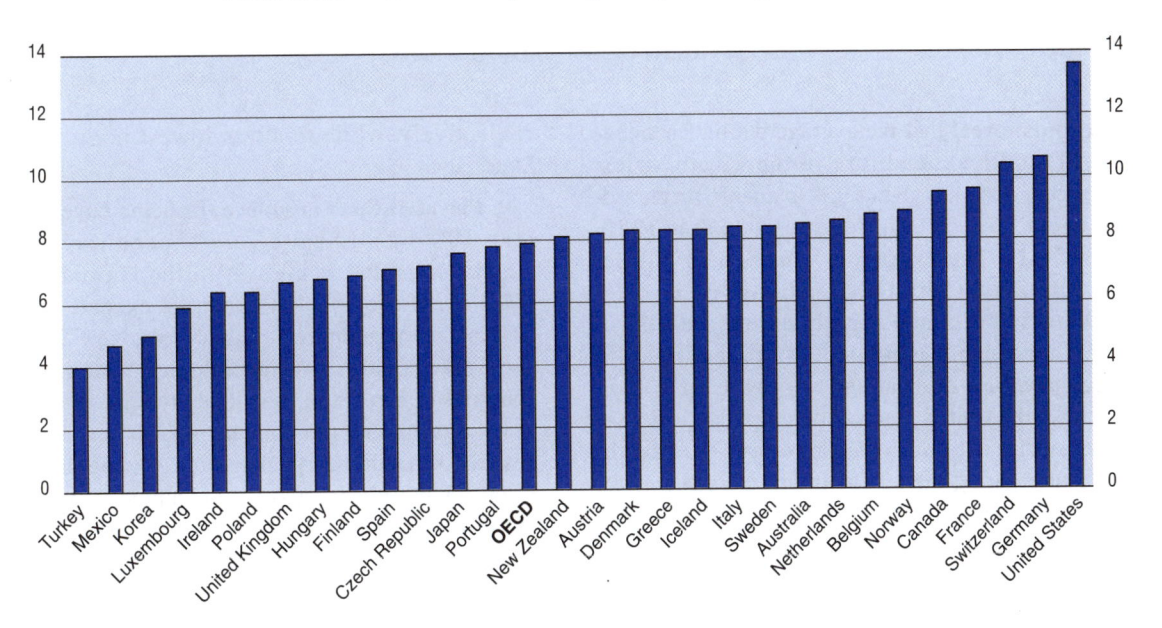

Source: OECD Health Data 2000.

Further reading

■ OECD (2000), *A System of Health Accounts*, Paris. ■ OECD (1999), *A Caring World: The New Social Policy Agenda*, Paris. ■ OECD (1994), *The Reform of Health Care Systems: A Review of Seventeen OECD Health Care Systems*, Paris. ■ OECD (1992), *The Reform of Health Care: A Comparative Analysis of Seven OECD Countries*, Paris.

© OECD 2001

C8. RESPONSIBILITY FOR FINANCING HEALTH CARE

Definition and measurement

Indicators of who pays for health care are important for equity and accessibility issues in health care: are populations sufficiently covered for health risks, do the poor have adequate access to medical services (B1, C1, C3)? Public funding of health care can be financed through central, state or local taxation as well as contributions to social security and health insurance funds that are part of general government (A13). Private funding of health care can take different forms: direct financing by individuals through so-called "out-of pocket payments", financing by private health insurance funds, enterprise-financed medical facilities, payments by charities and direct private investment in health facilities. Insofar as private financing of health care expenditure is subject to interpersonal re-distribution (either through government price-setting financing, mandating participation in private health programmes or the provisions of favourable tax treatment), it is a form of social expenditure (Adema, 1999).

Information on private financing of health care is not available for all countries. Furthermore, "out-of pocket" expenditure cannot (as yet) be separated into a) the complete individual financing of a medical service/product, and b), individual financing of medical interventions that are partly covered by public and private health insurance systems: so-called "co-payments".

Evidence and explanations

Trends reveal that the average public financed share of health expenditure in the 22 countries for which a complete data set is available increased from about 70% in 1970 to around 75% in 1980 (Chart C8.1). The average proportion of public financing across the OECD stabilised during the 1980s, and declined slightly during the 1990s, and this tendency was particularly pronounced in Greece, Italy, New Zealand, and Norway (Chart C8.1). In contrast, the United States experienced an increase in the public financing component of health expenditure during the 1990s. In all, there seems to be a convergence in the relative importance of financing components of health care expenditure across the OECD (C7).

Nevertheless, **cross-country variation** in public and private financing shares remains considerable (Chart C8.2). In 1998, Luxembourg and the Czech Republic reported the highest public financing share of health expenditure at 92.3% and 91.9% respectively, while this was lowest in the United States at 44.7%.

Private health insurance financing covers more than 10% of all health care expenditure in the Netherlands and is highest in the United States (32.4%). Out-of-pocket expenses exceed 20% of health care expenditure in Italy, Korea, New Zealand, and Turkey, and is considerable in a wide range of countries (Chart C8.2). It is likely that much of these individual payments concern health services not covered in insurance packages (*e.g.* some dentistry services), but it is impossible to be precise on this in the absence of information on co-payments.

Status indicators: Life expectancy (C1), Potential years of life lost (C3).
Response indicators: Tax wedge (A13), Public social expenditure (B6), Private social expenditure (B7), Health care expenditure (C7), Health infrastructure (C9).

C8. RESPONSIBILITY FOR FINANCING HEALTH CARE

Chart C8.1. **Evolution in the public financing share of health expenditure (1970-1998)**

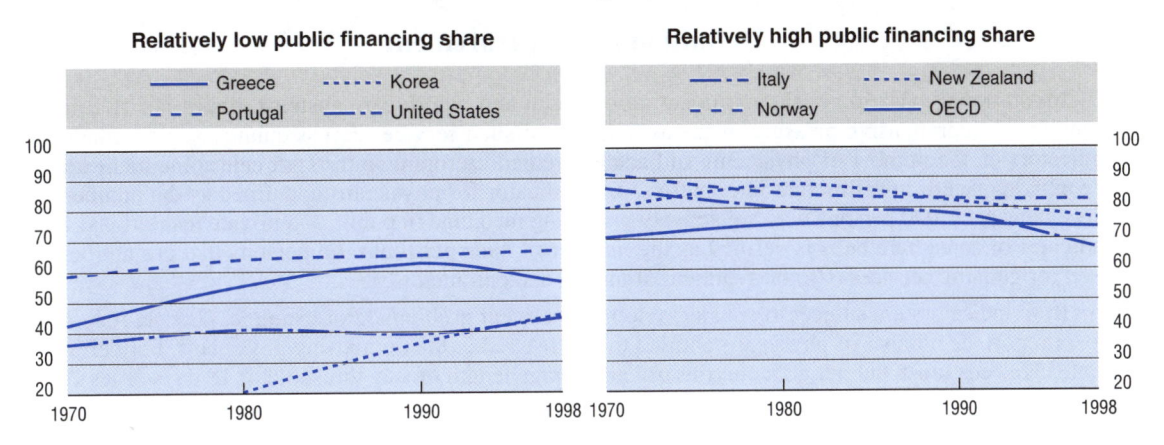

Relatively low public financing share: Greece, Korea, Portugal, United States

Relatively high public financing share: Italy, New Zealand, Norway, OECD

Chart C8.2. **Financing and change in public share of health expenditure**

Distribution of financing — Share of total health expenditure
- Public funding
- Private insurance
- Out-of-pocket payments

Change in public financing from 1970 to 1997 — Percentage points

Countries (top to bottom): Korea, United States, Greece, Mexico, Portugal, Italy, Australia, Canada, Netherlands, Austria, Poland, Turkey, Ireland, Hungary, Finland, France, Spain, Germany, New Zealand, Japan, Denmark, Norway, United Kingdom, Iceland, Sweden, Belgium, Czech Republic, Luxembourg

Turkey: 37; Korea: 34 (n.a. for Mexico, Poland, Hungary, Denmark)

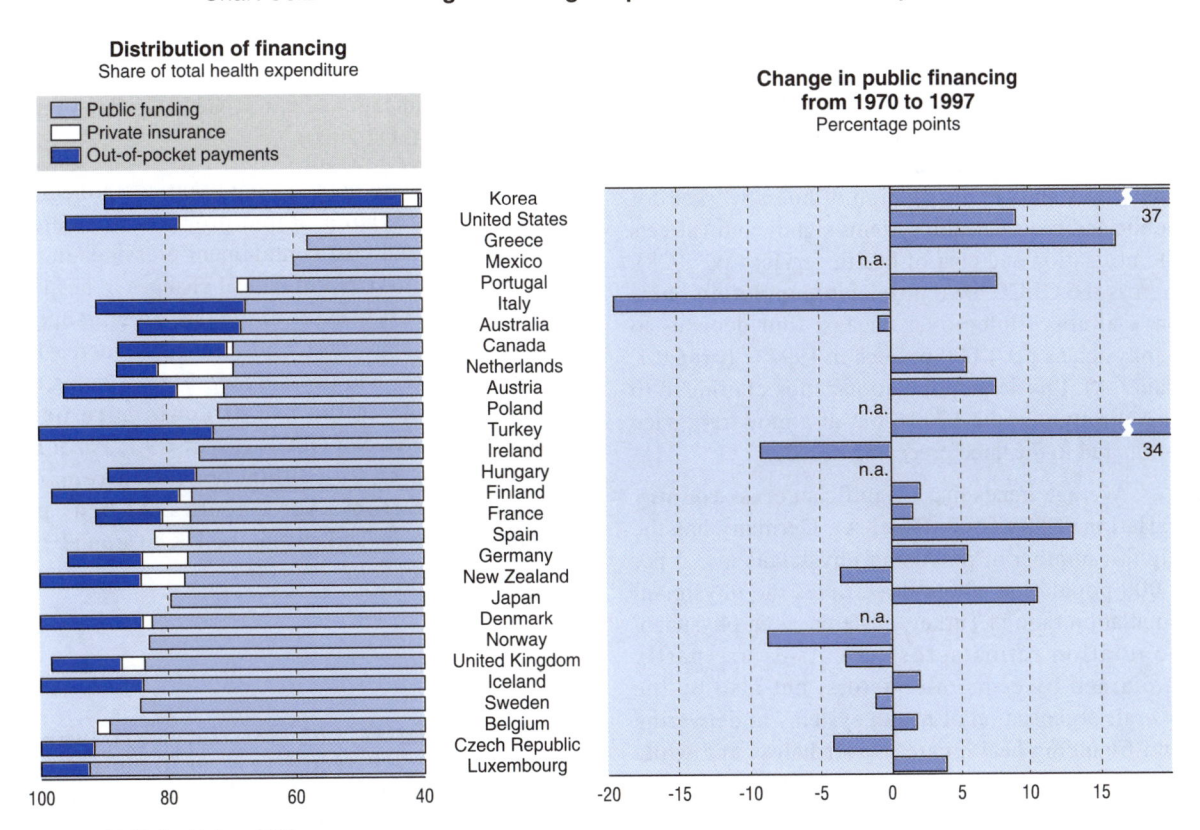

Source: OECD Health Data 2000.

Further reading

- Adema, W. (1999), "Net total social expenditure", Labour Market and Social Policy Occasional Paper, No. 39, OECD, Paris.

© OECD 2001

C9. HEALTH INFRASTRUCTURE

Definition and measurement

Institutional variation in the organisation of social and health care systems makes it difficult to provide a comprehensive measure of the availability of such services across countries. Nevertheless, indicators on the number of physicians and acute care beds across countries provide some measure of the existing health infrastructure in countries. The indicator for physicians is defined as the number of physicians per 1 000 persons who are actively practising medicine in public and private institutions. The indicator of acute care beds is defined as the number of beds per thousand persons that are not being used for geriatric services (C6) or treatment of mental and chronic diseases.

Both indicators are subject to considerable measurement problems. For example, Greece, Italy and Spain report the number of physicians entitled to practise rather than practising physicians. For defining acute care beds most, but not all, countries use an average length of stay threshold of 18 days or less.

Evidence and explanations

Physicians, including both hospital doctors and general practitioners are the primary resource for producing health care. Hence, the number of physicians and the distribution of hours worked for public and private health systems significantly affects the utilisation and cost of health services (C7, C8). Across the OECD area, **physician/population** ratios have almost tripled over the last four decades to 3 physicians per 1 000 persons in 1997 (Chart C9.1, Panel A). Physician/population ratios continued to rise throughout the 1990s, but at a moderate pace compared to the three preceding decades.

Average trends mask significant **cross-country** variation (Chart C9.2, Panel A). Germany has the highest number of practising physicians at 3.5 per 1 000 population, about three times the physician/population ratio in Turkey. Differences in physician/population ratios across countries are partly explained by economic factors, but also by the overall organisation of health systems in delivering and financing health care. Nevertheless and while controlling for other determinants of health outcomes, empirical evidence strongly suggests that increasing physician/population ratios are correlated with lower mortality (C1, C2, C3 – Grubaugh and Santerre, 1994; Or, 2000).

Hospitals are another important component of health care provision. Rapid progress in medical technologies and cost containment pressures in the past 30 years, have led to radical changes in hospital operations with greater emphasis on enhancing efficiency through shorter hospital stays, increasing patient turnover and day-surgery. This explains the steady decline in the use of **acute care beds** since 1980 across the OECD (Chart C9.1, Panel B). Nevertheless cross-country variation remains considerable from over 2 acute care beds per 1 000 persons in Turkey and the UK to around 7 in Germany (Chart C9.2, Panel B).

Status indicators: Life expectancy (C1), Infant mortality (C2), Potential years of life lost (C3).
Response indicators: Older people in institutions (C6), Health care expenditure (C7), Responsibility for financing health care (C8).

C9. HEALTH INFRASTRUCTURE

Chart C9.1. **Evolution of the number of practising physicians and acute care beds per 1 000 population (1960-1998)**

A. Practising physicians

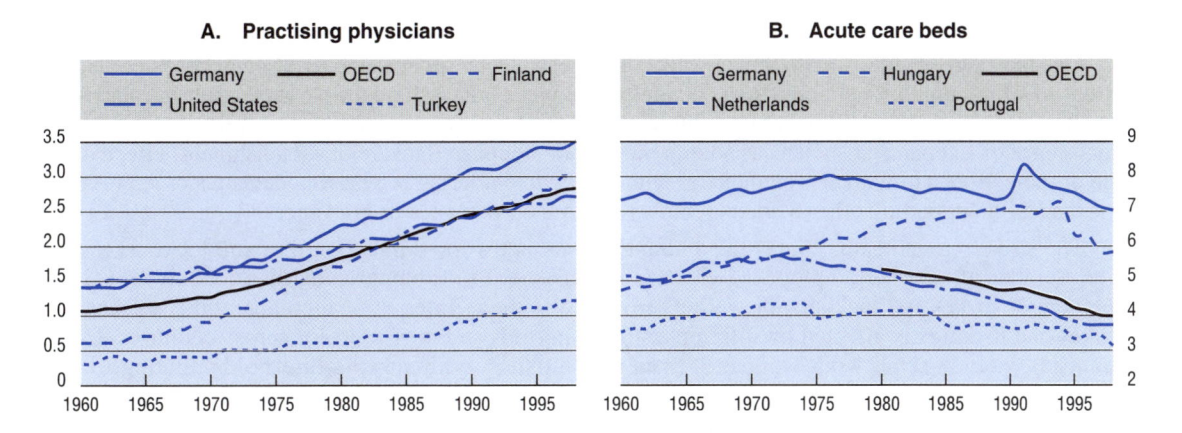

B. Acute care beds

Chart C9.2. **Practising physicians and acute care beds per 1 000 population, late 1990s**

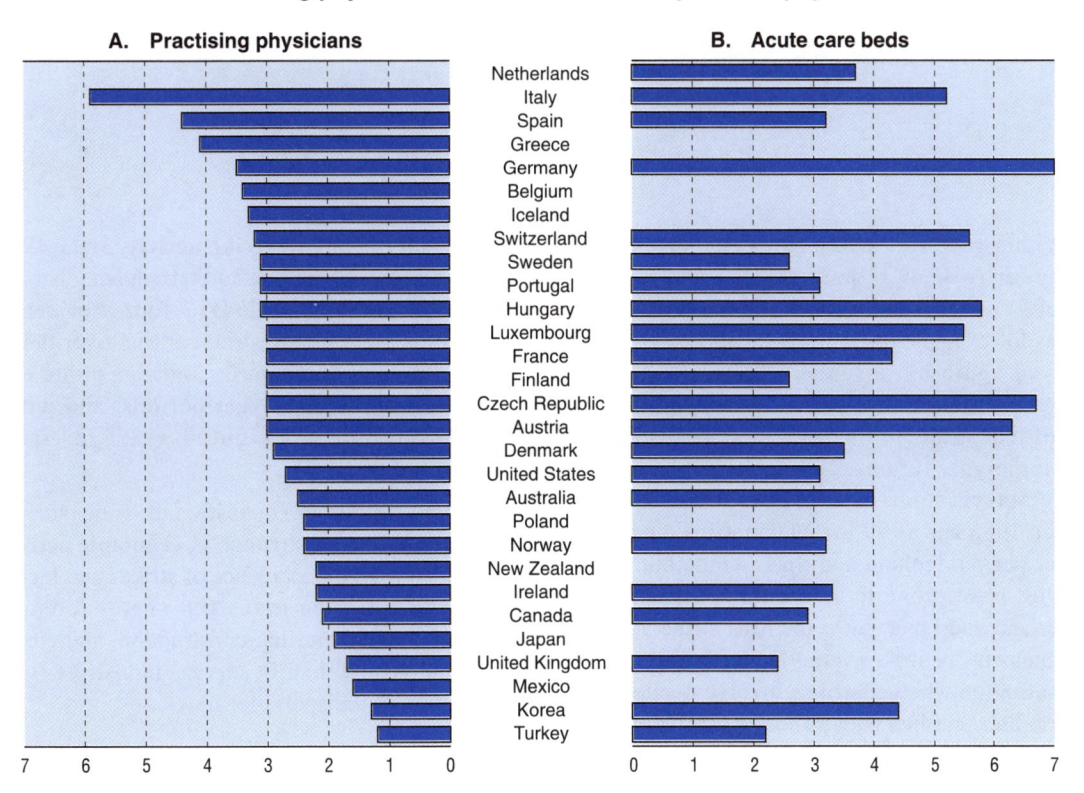

A. Practising physicians

B. Acute care beds

Source: OECD Health Data 2000.

Further reading

- Grubaugh, S.G. and R.E. Santerre (1994), "Comparing the performance of health-care systems: An alternative approach", *Southern Economic Journal*, 60, (4), pp. 1030-1042. ■ Or, Z. (2000), "Exploring the effects of health care on mortality across OECD countries", Labour Market and Social Policy Occasional Papers, No. 46, OECD, Paris.

D1. STRIKES

Definition and measurement

One indicator of strains in the relationships between societal groups, and thus social cohesion, is the extent to which employment conflicts between employees, unions and employers result in industrial conflict such as strikes and lockouts. A strike (lockout) has been defined by the ILO's International Conference of Labour Statisticians as a temporary work stoppage (closure of establishment) effected by one or more groups of workers (employers) with a view to enforcing or resisting demands or expressing grievances, or supporting other workers (employers) in their demands or grievances.

The strike rate indicator relates the amount of time not worked due to strikes and lockouts to the total number of salaried employees, which is better suited for comparisons than to show absolute numbers of strikes and lockouts, or workers involved in them. International comparability of data on strikes and lockouts is affected by differences in definitions and measurement across countries. Most countries exclude small work stoppages from the statistics, with varying thresholds relating to the number of workers involved and/or the number of days lost. Other countries may not include stoppages in particular industries (such as the public sector), political strikes or "wildcat" strikes in their official records. Countries may also omit workers indirectly involved (those who are unable to work because others at their workplace are on strike) or work stoppages indirectly caused (because of shortage of materials supplied by enterprises subject to strike activity).

Evidence and explanations

Within countries **strike rates** can vary wildly from year to year (Chart D1.1). A normally "peaceful" country may show a sudden peak in one year (as for example in Denmark in 1985 and 1998), followed again by absence of activity. Hence, averages over longer time-periods portray a country's level of industrial conflict in a more realistic way than single-year figures, and Table D1.1 presents rolling six-year period averages for the period between 1988 and 1999 for 26 countries. Over this 12-year period, Iceland and Spain come out as the countries most prone to industrial conflict, while Switzerland and Japan show the least strike activity. The "intensity" of strikes varies from case to case but information on whether strikes involve occupations of work-sites, clashes with police or arrests of trade unionists is not available across countries on a comprehensive basis.

While showing the considerable year-to-year variation in rates of conflict, Chart D1.1 illustrates the **trend decline in strike activity** since 1980, the Netherlands and the United States having persistently low strike activity. Table D1.1 further evidences the overall decline in industrial conflict over the 1990s, with only 7 of 26 countries showing a rate increase between the two six-year periods, and with both weighted and unweighted averages trending downward.

In a number of countries, labour disputes can be further analysed by **branch of economic activity**. As a general rule, the incidence of strikes and lockouts is higher within the industrial sector (comprising mining, manufacturing, construction, and electricity, gas and water) than in service industries (with the exception of transportation).

Status indicators: Employment (A1), Group membership (D5).

D1. STRIKES

Chart D1.1. Evolution of days lost through industrial action per 1 000 workers in selected OECD countries, 1980-1999

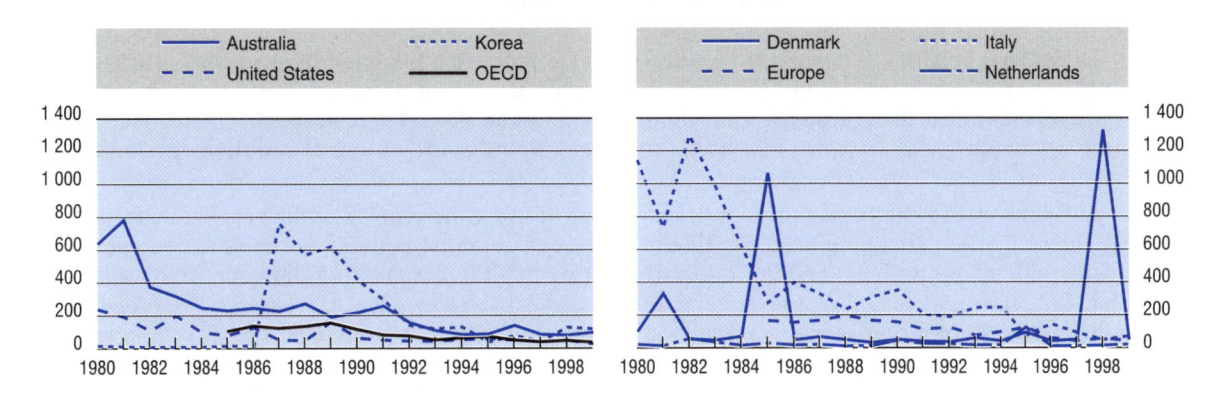

Table D1.1. Days lost through industrial action per 1 000 salaried employees, 1988-1999

	Years 1988	Years 1998	Years 1999	Averages 1988-99	Averages 1988-93	Averages 1994-99
Switzerland	0	7	1	1	0	2
Japan	4	2	0	3	3	2
Austria	3	0	0	4	6	1
Luxembourg	3	0	0	9	8	10
Germany	2	1	2	9	15	4
Netherlands	2	5	11	19	14	24
Belgium	66	28	8	34	42	26
Portugal	67	28	20	42	60	23
Poland	24	4	10	42	71	14
United States	42	42	16	50	61	39
United Kingdom	168	12	10	54	87	20
Sweden	199	0	22	66	93	40
Norway	45	141	3	72	60	84
France	107	51	64	86	80	92
New Zealand	313	9	12	94	160	27
Ireland	172	32	168	118	145	90
Australia	265	72	88	140	193	87
Denmark	41	1 317	38	147	35	258
Finland	88	70	10	155	152	158
Italy	226	40	62	175	246	103
Korea	562	119	109	216	353	80
Turkey	266	31	26	222	322	123
Canada	423	207	200	248	282	214
Greece	505	19	1	322	614	29
Spain	1 399	127	139	421	589	253
Iceland	927	555	0	442	284	600
Averages						
OECD (weighted)	135	48	37	76	102	52
OECD (unweighted)	228	112	39	123	153	92
OECD Europe (weighted)	187	49	32	94	129	61

Source: ILO (2001).

Further reading
- ILO (2001), *Yearbook of Labour Statistics 2000,* International Labour Office, Geneva.

D2. DRUG USE AND RELATED DEATHS

Definition and measurement

Drug abuse is both a symptom and a cause of social problems. Escaping from stresses of life can lead to a risk of addiction, in turn reducing the chances of holding down a decent job, maintaining family relationships. Illicit drug use is also linked with crime (D4). These problems often concern a relatively small group of "problem users" that face a multitude of social problems including homelessness.

Indicators used here include the annual prevalence of use as percentage of the population aged 15 and above. These data come from confidential surveys amongst people, and are thus subject to considerable response bias, and do not easily distinguish the casual irregular user from addicts (Chart D2.1). Drug-related deaths are a cause of grave social concern. Chart D2.2 presents information on the number drug-related deaths per 1 million persons. In the EU countries, statistics on drug-related deaths generally refer to deaths occurring shortly after drug use (acute intoxication, overdose, poisoning or drug-induced deaths). However, a direct comparison between national statistics is difficult because of the variety of reporting systems and definitions. Bearing this in mind, drug-related deaths can be an indicator of trends for severe forms of drug use.

Evidence and explanations

The most used substances are cannabis, amphetamines, opiates, ecstasy, and cocaine, and the risk drug-related deaths varies with the substance and the pattern of use. Cannabis continues to be, by far, the most widely consumed drug world wide. In fact, information on trends for substances other than cannabis is more limited and difficult to interpret.

The use of **cannabis and amphetamines** is rising in most OECD countries and is highest in Australia, New Zealand and the United States, while Japan and Korea having the lowest use. (Chart D2.1). Cannabis consumption is rising in Europe except for Ireland and the UK (EMCDDA, 1999). Strikingly, surveys amongst Dutch secondary education students reveal that cannabis use more than quadrupled between 1984 and 1998, with use of cannabis among boys almost twice as high than among girls.

Trends in **drug-related deaths** differ from country to country, perhaps as a result of changes in recording procedures (Chart D2.2). Despite these limitations, until the mid-1990s the number of drug-related deaths generally increased, but since then national trends have become diverse. In many countries, the number of drug-related deaths has stabilised (*e.g.* Denmark and the UK) or even decreased (*e.g.* Austria, Italy, and Luxembourg) (see the annex on Internet).

In a few countries, the trend is still upwards, especially in those where opiate use appears to have spread more recently as in Greece, Ireland and Portugal. Apart from these countries, the stabilisation in drug-related deaths may be explained by a stabilisation in "problematic" **drug-use** prevalence, to changes in patterns of use (such as a decrease in injecting) or to the effects of interventions (like the spread of opiate substitution programmes).

Status indicators: Potential years of life lost (C3), Suicide rates (D3).
Response indicators: Health care expenditure (C7), Prisoners (D7).

D2. DRUG USE AND RELATED DEATHS

Chart D2.1. Annual prevalence of use of cannabis and amphetamines, 1999

As a percentage of the population aged 15 and above

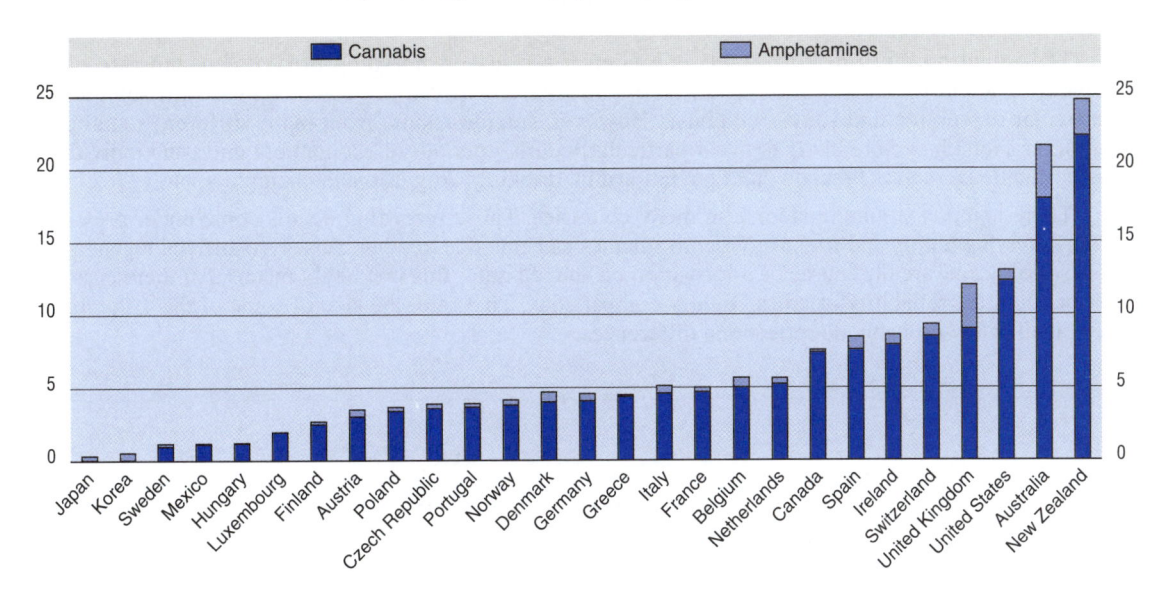

Source: UNDCP (2000).

Chart D2.2. Drug-related deaths in selected countries, 1985-1997

Mortality per 1 000 000 people

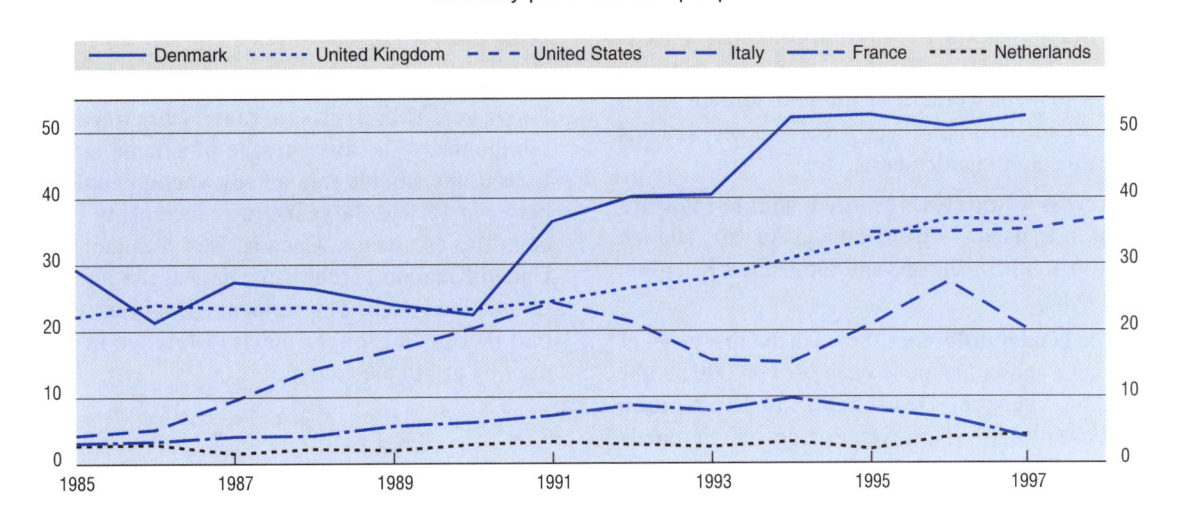

Source: EMCDDA (1999), UN (1999) and SAMSHA (2001).

Further reading

- EMCDDA (1999), *Extended Annual Report on the State of the Drugs Problem in European Union*, European Ministerial Conference for Drugs and Drug Addiction, Brussels. ■ SAMSHA (2001), www.samsha.gov, Substance Abuse and Mental Health Services Administration, US. ■ Trimbos Institute (2001), Policy briefs and Fact sheets, www.trimbos.nl, Netherlands Institute for Mental Health and Addiction. ■ UN (1999), *World Population Prospects: The 1998 Revision*, United Nations, New York. ■ UNDCP (2000), *Global Illicit Drug Trends*, United Nations International Drug Control Programme, New York.

D3. SUICIDE

Definition and measurement

The intentional killing of oneself is evidence not just of personal breakdown, but also says something about social conditions. Mental disorders are involved in 90% of all cases of suicide, in particular depression and substance abuse. However, suicide results from many different social and cultural factors: it is more likely to occur particularly during periods of economic, family and individual crisis situations, such as breakdown of a relationship, drinking, drug use, and unemployment.

There is much stigma in suicide in many countries. Those recording deaths come under pressure from surviving family and friends to record suicides as being due to other causes. As official registers of "causes of death' are the source of information on suicide rates, this inevitably means that there is some doubt about the reliability of cross-country comparisons. That said, the size of some of the differences described below probably do reflect real differences.

Evidence and explanations

Whilst it is never possible to separate out the contributing social factors from the personal desperation that leads to suicide, few could doubt that it is sometimes a response to social problems such as drug use (D2) and unemployment (A2). In the last 30 years, suicide rates have increased by more than 10% on average among the OECD countries (Chart D3.1, Panel A). However, from the early 1980s (for women) or the mid- to late 1980s (for men), the **trend** has been towards a very gradual improvement in suicide rates.

Across countries, recorded suicide rates are highest in Finland, Switzerland and Austria, and are lowest in southern Europe and the United Kingdom (Chart D3.2).

The **gender difference** shown in the first panel of Chart D3.1 shows that male rates per 100 000 people were, on average, 10 higher than for women from 1960 onwards. However, as a decline in female suicides which began in about 1980, preceded a later decline for men, the difference between the genders has been increasing for the last 15 years, and has now reached about 14 per 100 000 persons. Generally, if a country has a high male suicide rate in comparison with other countries, then it will also have a high female suicide rate. Female suicides in Japan and Denmark are more common than might have been expected, given their male suicide rates, the opposite being true for Poland.

Suicide rates rise with **age** (Chart D3.1, Panel B). However, this stylised fact is becoming less pronounced. The average age of suicide is falling. Indeed, the suicide rate among young people (aged between 15 and 34 years) was increasing in some countries (Australia, Canada, New Zealand and the United Kingdom) at the same time as the suicide rate of the elderly fell. This tendency has been so strong that there is no longer much difference in suicide rates by age in these countries.

Status indicators: Unemployment (A2), Potential years of life lost (C3), Drug use and related deaths (D2).

D3. SUICIDE

Chart D3.1. **Suicide rate by gender and by age, per 100 000 persons (average of 21 countries)**

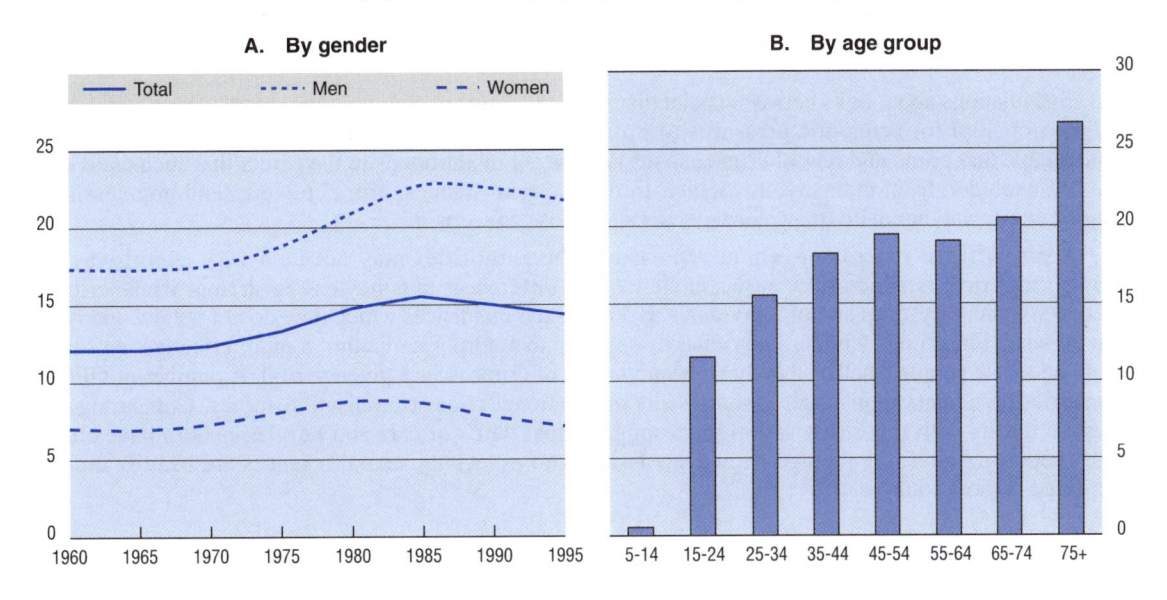

A. By gender

B. By age group

Chart D3.2. **Suicide rate per 100 000 persons by gender, 1995**

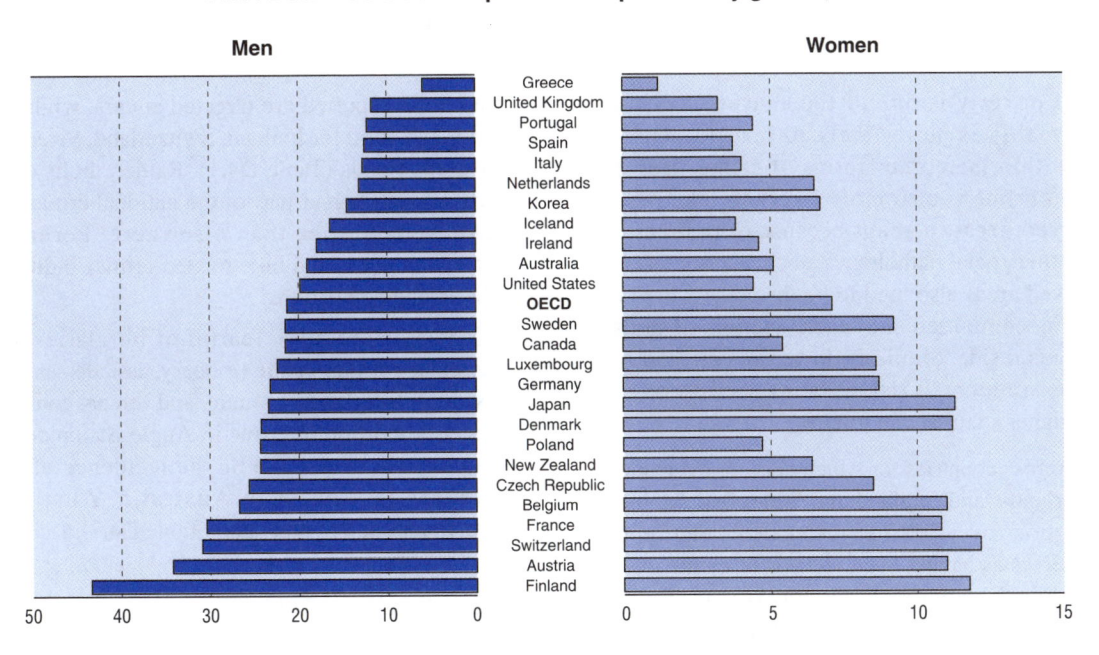

Source: World Health Organisation (2001).

Further reading

- World Health Organisation (2001), Mental health project on suicide prevention named "Live your life"; Data available on: http://www.who.int/mental_health/Topic_Suicide/suicide1.html

D4. CRIME

Definition and measurement

Speculations about links between social distress and crime are commonplace, particularly in relation to the potential for economic pressures to provide an incentive for theft. Whatever the cause, it is undeniable that crime and fear of crime can destabilise neighbourhoods to the extent that such areas can be left excluded from mainstream society. In these circumstances, crime, poverty and hopelessness reinforce one another, with tragic consequences for those concerned.

Using official records of crimes reported to the authorities may not be a very useful way of comparing crime rates across countries in view of the differences in policy on registering "trivial crime" between judicial systems and of individuals to report such incidences which they do not believe likely to be pursued. For crimes with an individual as opposed to a corporate victim, a more effective approach may be to ask people whether they have been victims of crime over a given period. A number of OECD countries participate in just such a study – the international crime victimisation survey. Comparing the survey results with reported crime figures suggests that thefts of cars and burglaries both have about 80% reporting rates, on average. However, assault and especially sexual offences are heavily under-reported in most countries.

Evidence and explanations

If poverty is one of the causes of crime, it presumably is more likely to lead to crimes of acquisition than other forms of crime. However, violent crime is also more likely to take place in **deprived areas**, perhaps because of indirect links with other social pathologies, such as drug use (D2). Deprived areas also tend to be the areas where most crime is committed and where victims of multiple incidents reside. Similarly, lower income and status groups are more at risk of being victims of crime than higher status social groups.

Across countries for which data are available, the Netherlands, and England and Wales had the highest proportion (over 30%) of respondents that reported themselves as having been **victims of crime** over the preceding 12 months. Rates for Austria, Belgium, Finland, Northern Ireland and Sweden were below 20% in the mid-1990s (Chart D4.1).

Car-related crimes are the most common, either damage or theft. In France, England and Wales, half of the crimes reported are targeted at cars, while this is less than a third for Finland, Switzerland, Sweden, and the Netherlands (Table D4.1). Rather, thefts of bikes form a much bigger part of the national crime picture in these countries than elsewhere. Perhaps not surprisingly, car and bike related crimes induce little fear among populations.

People are more fearful of burglaries and in particular **contact crime** (robbery, assaults and sexual assaults). Burglaries, assaults and threats constitute a bigger proportion of crime in Anglo-Saxon countries than anywhere else, while the incidence of sexual offences is highest in Australia, Austria, the Netherlands and Switzerland (Table D4.2).

Status indicators: Relative poverty (B1), Drug use and related deaths (D2).
Response indicators: Prisoners (D7).

D4. CRIME

Chart D4.1. Proportion of respondents who were victims of crime in a given year

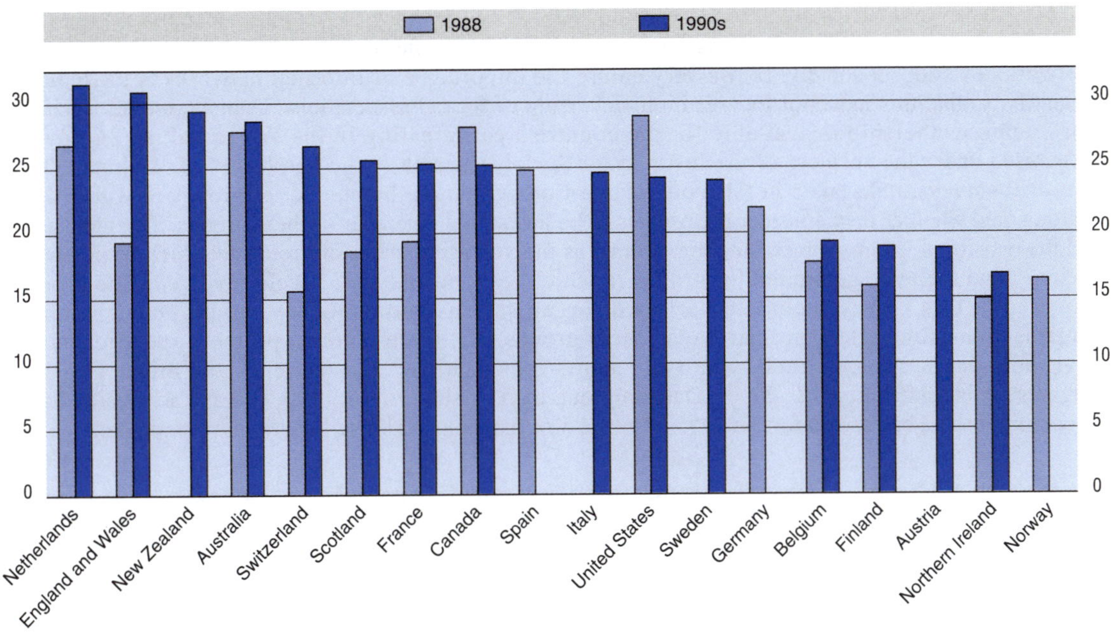

[Bar chart comparing 1988 vs 1990s victimisation rates across countries: Netherlands, England and Wales, New Zealand, Australia, Switzerland, Scotland, France, Canada, Spain, Italy, United States, Sweden, Germany, Belgium, Finland, Austria, Northern Ireland, Norway]

Table D4.1. **Vehicle-related crime as a proportion of crimes reported by vehicle owners in 1995**

	Car damage	Car theft	Theft from car	Motorcycle theft	Bicycle theft
Finland	4.3	0.4	2.9	0.2	5.1
Sweden	4.6	1.2	4.9	0.5	8.8
Belgium (1991)	6.1	1.0	3.9	1.1	2.8
Canada	6.2	1.5	6.2	0.1	3.3
Austria	6.7	0.1	1.6	0.0	3.3
Northern Ireland	6.7	1.6	3.1	..	1.2
United States	6.7	1.9	7.5	0.2	3.3
Switzerland	7.1	0.1	3.0	1.4	7
Italy (1991)	7.6	2.7	7.0	1.5	2.3
New Zealand (1991)	7.9	2.7	6.9	0.3	4.4
France	8.3	1.6	7.2	0.8	2.8
Australia (1991)	9.5	3.1	6.6	0.3	2.1
Scotland	9.8	1.7	6.6	0.1	1.9
Netherlands	9.9	0.4	5.4	0.7	9.5
England and Wales	10.4	2.5	8.1	0.2	3.5

Table D4.2. **Contact crime and burglaries as a proportion of all incidents reported by respondents in 1995**

	Assault and threat	Sexual offences	Burglary	Robbery
Italy (1991)	0.8	1.7	2.4	1.3
Northern Ireland	1.7	1.2	1.5	0.5
Belgium (1991)	1.8	1.4	2.1	1.0
Austria	2.1	3.8	0.9	0.2
Switzerland	3.1	4.6	1.3	0.9
France	3.9	0.9	2.3	1.0
Canada	4.0	2.7	3.4	1.2
Netherlands	4.0	3.6	2.6	0.6
Finland	4.1	2.5	0.6	0.5
Scotland	4.2	1.3	1.5	0.8
Sweden	4.5	2.9	1.3	0.5
Australia (1991)	4.7	3.5	3.7	1.3
United States	5.7	2.5	2.6	1.3
New Zealand (1991)	5.7	2.7	4.3	0.7
England and Wales	5.9	2.0	3.0	1.4

Source: van Dijk and Mayhew (1997).

Further reading

- Dijk, J.J.M. van and P. Mayhew (1997), *Criminal Victimisation in Eleven Industrialised Countries. Key Findings from the 1996 International Crime Victims Survey*, s-Gravenhage, Ministry of Justice, the Netherlands. ■ Data and methodological aspects of the International Crime Victim Survey can be found on: http://ruljis.leidenuniv.nl/group/jfcr/www/icvs/backindex.htm; United Nations Crime and Justice Information Network: http://www.uncjin.org/.

D5. GROUP MEMBERSHIP

Definition and measurement

One aspect of social cohesion is the extent to which people participate in formal and informal networks existing in society. By its very nature the importance of informal networks is difficult to quantify, so that this indicator focuses on membership of formal associations. Comparable information on group-membership is available for the countries participating in the World Values Survey as organised under the auspices of the Institute for Social Research of the University of Michigan. The national surveys undertaken in this context question people on the number of groups to which they belong, and whether they consider themselves to be an "active" member of these groups. The indicators on the density of group-membership are defined as the average number of groups to which respondents belong, and the average number of groups in which respondents are actively involved. The groups covered in this survey include a variety of organisations and advocacy groups. For example, organisations aiming to serve particular client groups (*e.g.* trade unions), promote specific causes (*e.g.* political parties), cultural, youth and sports organisations, and churches and other religious organisations (Inglehart *et al.*, 2000). Data on group membership for the 1990-91 wave are available on a comprehensive basis, data for the 1995-97 wave have become available but are less comprehensive.

Evidence and explanations

To a considerable extent **cross-country differences** in the density of associational activity are historically determined. In societies where membership of a single group can affect various aspects of societal life, or where the role of informal networks is relatively strong, individuals have fewer reasons to belong to different groups at the same time. Traditionally, civil society involvement in public life is strongest in Nordic countries, the Netherlands, and to a somewhat lesser extent in Canada and the United States. On average Dutchmen and Icelanders are member of at least 2 groups, while only 2 out of 5 Spaniards consider themselves as member of a formal group (Chart D5.1).

Group-membership as such says little about the **intensity** with which people **participate** in associations. On average, about 1 in 2 people actively participates in one organisation or another, with Canada, Finland and the United States being above this norm. In countries with the highest density of group membership (Denmark, the Netherlands, Norway, Sweden and Iceland), people are only actively participant in 1 out of 4 of the organisations to which they belong. In countries with a relatively low density of group membership, active group participation is far more likely, except in Hungary and Spain (Chart D5.1).

Membership of organisations that can advance and/or protect individual's economic and employment-related interests (*e.g.* unions, professional associations, and political parties), is more often associated with the working-age population than with other age-groups (A1, D1). Indeed, prime age persons are more likely to belong to groups than senior citizens, but not in France, Finland and the Netherlands. Group membership is slightly more prevalent among men than women, but increased female labour force participation is likely to further diminish this gender-gap (Chart D5.2).

Status indicators: Employment (A1), Strikes (D1).

D5. GROUP MEMBERSHIP

Chart D5.1. **Density of associational activity, 1990-1991**

- Average number of groups to which respondents belong
- ◆ Average number of groups in which respondents are active members

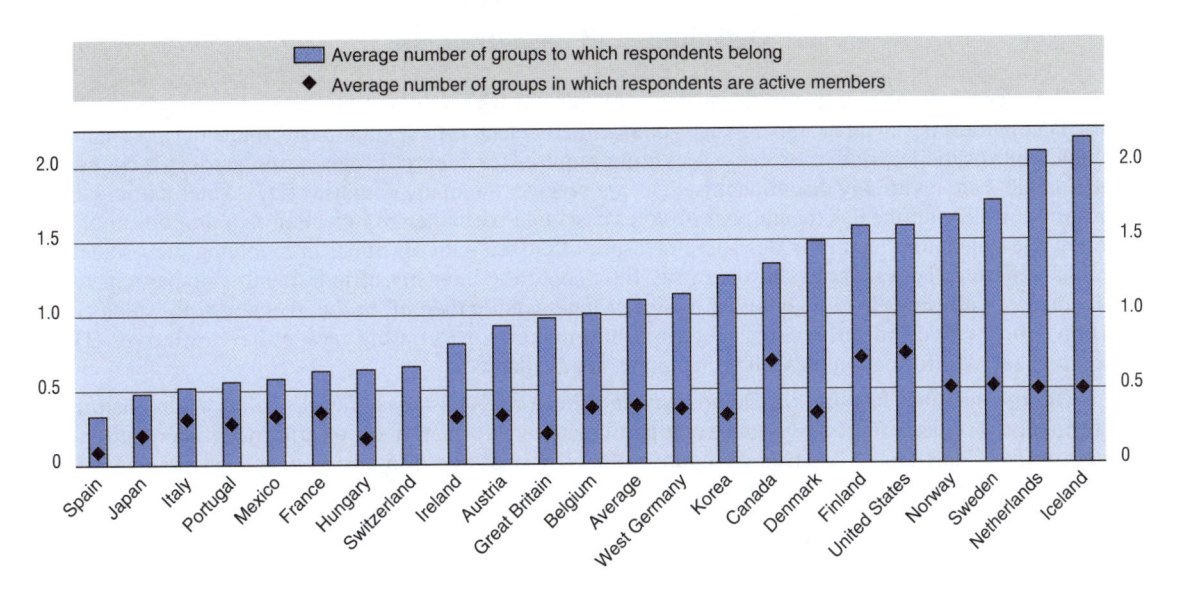

Countries (left to right): Spain, Japan, Italy, Portugal, Mexico, France, Hungary, Switzerland, Ireland, Austria, Great Britain, Belgium, Average, West Germany, Korea, Canada, Denmark, Finland, United States, Norway, Sweden, Netherlands, Iceland

Chart D5.2. **Average number of groups to which respondents belong by age and gender, 1990/91**

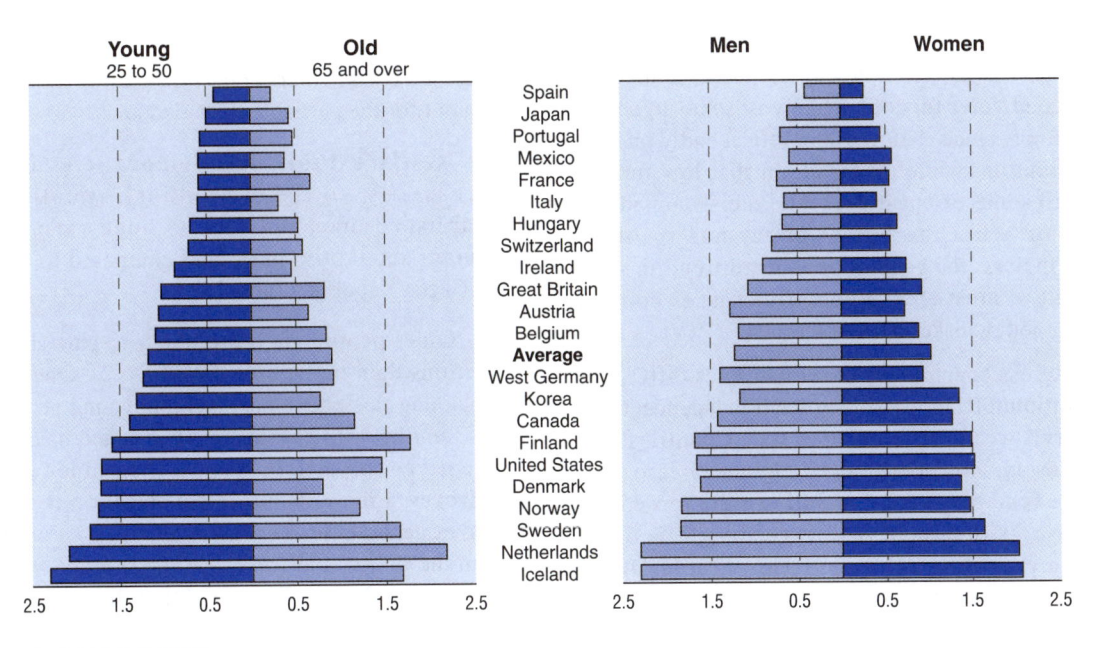

Young (25 to 50) / Old (65 and over) — Men / Women

Countries: Spain, Japan, Portugal, Mexico, France, Italy, Hungary, Switzerland, Ireland, Great Britain, Austria, Belgium, **Average**, West Germany, Korea, Canada, Finland, United States, Denmark, Norway, Sweden, Netherlands, Iceland

Source: Inglehart et al. (2000).

Further reading

- Knack, S. and P. Keefer (1997), "Does social capital have an economic payoff? A cross-country investigation", *The Quarterly Journal of Economics*, No. 112(4), pp. 1251-1288. ■ Inglehart, R, et al. (2000), *World Values Surveys and European Values Surveys*, 1981-1984, 1990-1993, and 1995-1997 [Computer file]. ICPSR version. Ann Arbor, MI: Institute for Social Research [producer], 2000. Ann Arbor, MI: Inter-university Consortium for Political and Social Research [distributor], 2000.

© OECD 2001

D6. VOTING

Definition and measurement

There are large differences in the ways and means in which democratic processes play out across OECD countries, but in all Member states voters directly elect, on a regular basis, (parts of) a parliament which controls the legislative process. As voting requires (residential) registration across all countries the homeless are invariably disenfranchised, as are prisoners in many countries (D7). Voter participation or turnout is here defined as the number of votes casts in a parliamentary election as a proportion of the voting age population, and provides some measure of citizen's involvement in moulding their societies and its cohesion. Turnout rates, however, say little about the intensity of individual civic participation, attendance of meetings held by political parties or membership thereof, or the intensity with which civic groups are involved in influencing (local) policy-makers or initiating new policy initiatives (D5). Comprehensive information on such indicators is not available.

The International Institute for Democracy and Electoral Assistance (IDEA) collates administrative information on electoral processes and voter participation. Information on voter turnout among different age groups (Chart D6.2) is based on country-specific post election surveys, and results can differ significantly from administrative data (IDEA, 1997).

Evidence and explanations

There is no commonly agreed benchmark as to what **good voter turnout** actually is: some argue that turnout rates much below 100% reflect badly on civic participation, while others claim that low turnout rates to some extent reveal the voter's considered view on what the ballot paper has to offer. Nevertheless, the general downward trend in voter turnout in most OECD countries causes concern among policy makers (Chart D6.1).

Across countries voter turnout rates differ with **institutional** factors, but they seem independent of a country's wealth or population size. Countries with compulsory voting (Australia, Belgium, Greece, Italy and Luxembourg) are generally in the top-end of countries with turnout rates exceeding 80% of the estimated voting age population (Table D6.1). However, the proportion of spoilt ballots is generally higher in these countries than elsewhere and exceeds 5% of all ballots in Belgium, Italy and Luxembourg. Electoral systems based on proportional representation that are more likely not to generate a two-party system have a somewhat higher voter turnout than systems based on "plurality/majority" voting (*e.g.* the "first past the post system"). Finally, as they can directly express their will through referenda Swiss voters appear difficult to motivate to turn out for the parliamentary elections.

Newly established democracies do not necessarily vote more enthusiastically than established ones and display huge variation in turnout: about 50% in Poland compared to 75% in the Czech Republic (Table D6.1).

Older people are more likely to participate in elections than the **young** (Chart D6.2). One theory explaining this phenomenon is that young people are less familiar with political processes and have fewer incentives to participate in it than older people. However, a more disturbing explanation is that the current generation of young voters feels so excluded from the political process that voter turnout will not increase with age. Support for either hypothesis requires information on voting behaviour of subsequent cohorts of young people which, unfortunately, is not available.

Status indicators: Group Membership (D5).
Response indicators: Prisoners (D7).

D6. VOTING

Chart D6.1. Voter turnout in parliamentary elections since 1960
Voter turnout as a percentage of the voting age population

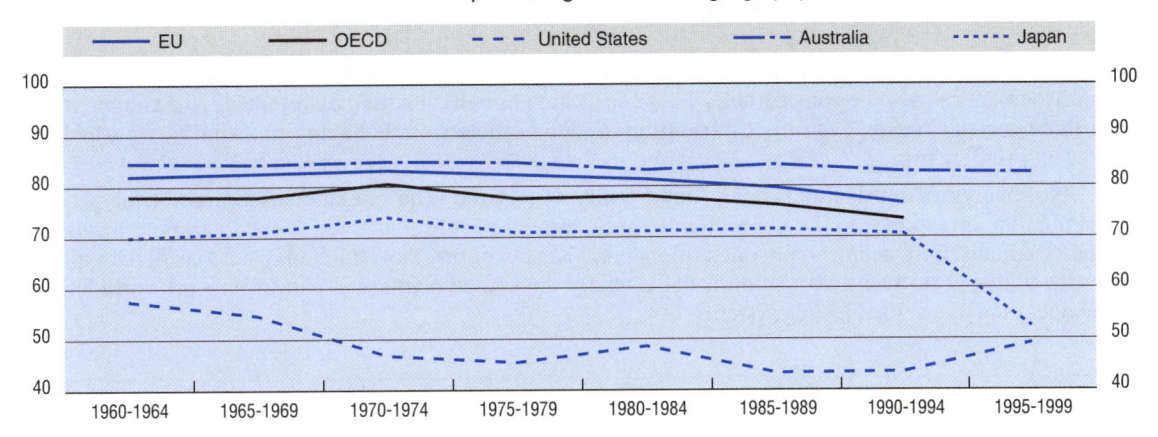

Chart D6.2. Turnout among first-time voters and voters aged 30 or older

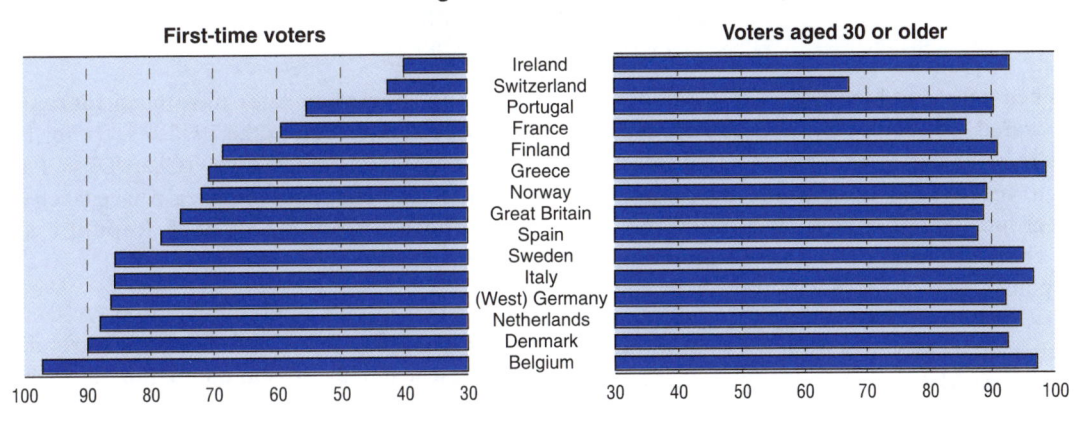

Source: IDEA (1999).

Table D6.1. Parliamentary elections and voter turnout as a percentage of the voting age population

	Number of elections since 1945	Year	Voter turnout		Number of elections since 1945	Year	Voter turnout
Switzerland	13	1995	35.7	Czech Republic	4	1998	76.7
Poland	4	1997	48.8	Norway	14	1997	76.9
United States	26	1996	49.1	Austria	16	1995	78.6
Mexico	18	1997	54.4	Portugal	9	1995	79.1
Canada	17	1997	56.2	Turkey	9	1995	79.1
Hungary	3	1998	59.4	Spain	7	1996	80.6
Japan	21	1996	59.8	Australia	21	1996	82.5
France	15	1997	59.9	New Zealand	18	1996	83
Luxembourg	12	1994	60.5	Denmark	22	1998	83.1
Korea	9	1996	65.3	Belgium	17	1995	83.2
Ireland	16	1997	66.7	Sweden	17	1994	83.6
United Kingdom	15	1997	69.4	Greece	17	1996	83.9
Finland	15	1995	71.1	Italy	14	1996	87.4
Germany	13	1994	72.4	Iceland	16	1995	87.8
Netherlands	15	1994	75.2				

Source: IDEA (1997).

Further reading

■ IDEA (1999), *Youth Voter Participation: Involving Today's Young in Tomorrow's Democracy*, International Institute for Democracy and Electoral Assistance, Stockholm.   ■ IDEA (1997), *Voter Turnout from 1947 to 1997: A Global Report on Political Participation*, International Institute for Democracy and Electoral Assistance, Stockholm (see also, http://www.idea.int).

D7. PRISONERS

Definition and measurement

Crime (D4) causes great suffering to victims and their families, but the costs associated with imprisonment can also be considerable. These costs are normally justified by reference to a combination of three societal "needs": to inflict retribution, to deter others from behaving in a similar way, and to prevent re-offending.

Not everyone in prison has been found guilty of a crime. The indicator used here of the prison population corresponds to the population of incarcerated people sentenced to incarceration, awaiting trial or adjudication, and/or imprisoned offenders, given as of one day which may be considered typical for the whole year. Such information is collected by the United Nations as part of its work considering the operation of criminal justice systems.

Evidence and explanations

When people at high risk of re-offending are incarcerated, the direct benefits are clear (D4). Where re-offending is unlikely, then consideration needs to be given to whether the retribution and deterrent functions of imprisonment justify the high direct **costs of** placing individuals into **custody**. Also, punishment of those who transgress societal rules does not finish with the end of a gaol term. Ex-convicts may be excluded from the right to vote in some countries (D6), and from certain social benefits in others (B6). Furthermore, whilst in gaol prisoners are likely to incur a loss of marketable skills and the prospects of finding an employer prepared to overlook a previous conviction can be low, making labour market reintegration of ex-convicts is a difficult challenge (A7).

Most **countries** incarcerate between 50 and 150 per 100 000 people at any point in time (Chart D7.1, Panel A). There are several exceptions: the Czech Republic having a higher ratio while Iceland, Japan and Norway fall below the norm. The most remarkable exception is the United States, where almost 550 people per 100 000 in gaol. Recent figures show that the total number of Americans being incarcerated is around 2 million, which compared with a labour force of around 120 million gives some perspective to the impressively low unemployment rate in the United States (A2).

Incarceration rates have been **increasing** in most countries during the 1990s except for Finland, Japan, Mexico and Norway (Chart D7.1, Panel B). Particularly high rates of increase have taken place in southern Europe, the Czech Republic and the Netherlands.

Those with limited education (A10), labour market difficulties and minorities are all over-represented in the **prison population** in countries for which such data exist. Some examples: in Ireland, it is estimated that 80% of the prison population left school before they were 16 (A3). The non-white prison population in the UK is 18% of the total number of male prisoners and 24% of the female total in 1997 compared to 6% in the England and Wales population as a whole. In the United States, it is estimated that the chances of someone born in 1991 being incarcerated at some point in their life is 29% for blacks, 4% for whites.

Status indicators: Unemployment (A2); Jobless youth (A3), Relative poverty (B1), Crime (D4), Voting (D6). **Response indicators**: Activation policies (A7), Educational attainment (A10), Public social expenditure (B6).

D7. PRISONERS

Chart D7.1. **Prison population indicators as a percentage of 100 000 persons**

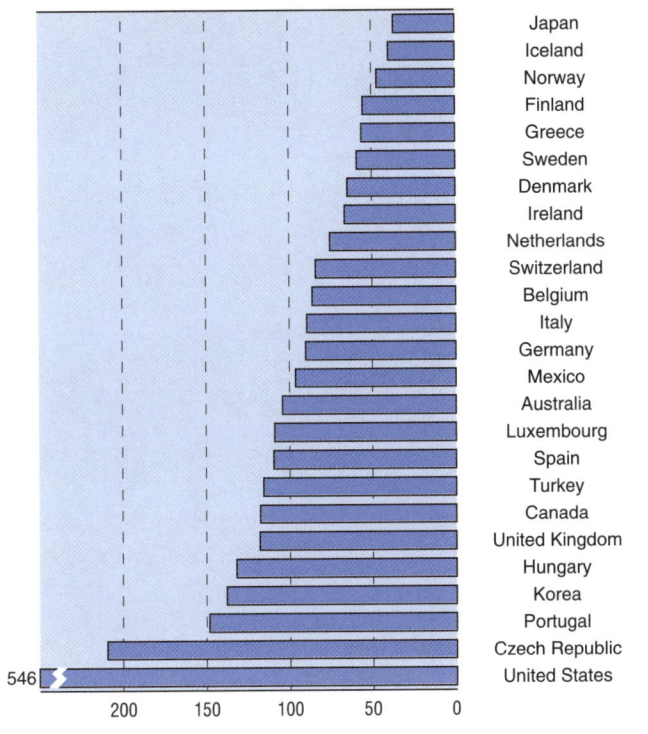

A. Incarceration rates 1997

B. Annual average in incarceration rates
In percentage point per year

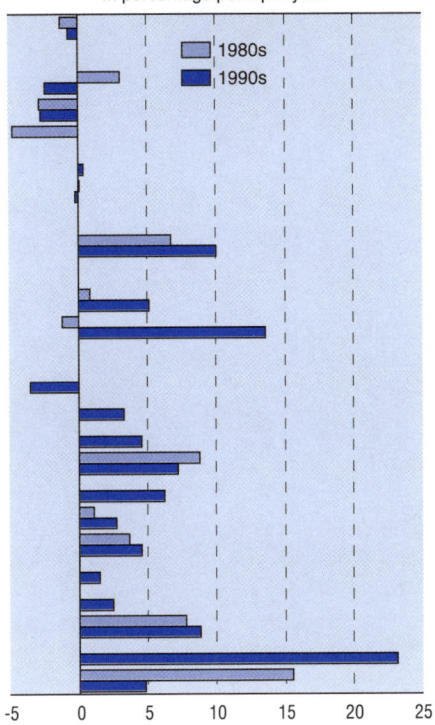

Source: UN (1997).

Further reading

- O'Mahony, P. (1997), *Mountjoy Prisoners: A Sociological and Criminological Profile*, Irish Ministry of Justice, Equality and Law Reform, Dublin. ■ United Nations (1997), *Survey on Crime Trends and the Operations of Criminal Justice Systems* (2nd to 6th surveys, 1975-1997), New York. ■ United Kingdom Home Office (1998), *Statistical Bulletin*, 5/98, London. ■ Schiraldi, V. and J. Ziedenberg (1999), *The Punishing Decade: Prison and Jail Estimates at the Millennium*, United States Justice Policy Institute, Washington.

© OECD 2001

111

OECD PUBLICATIONS, 2, rue André-Pascal, 75775 PARIS CEDEX 16
PRINTED IN FRANCE
(81 2001 06 1 P) ISBN 92-64-18674-3 – No. 51819 2001